Shaded by Stone

Shaded by Stone

Ari Schneider

Cover art by Devon Savino.
Interior art by Devon Savino and Ari Schneider.
Author photo by Kara Pearson.

Published by Xalibu Creative
Sioux Falls, SD

For inquiries:
contact@xalibucreative.com

ISBN: 978-1-7323482-3-3

For None

I stand before my highest mountain and my longest wandering: therefore I must descend deeper than I have ever descended.

—Thus Spoke Zarathustra

CONTENTS

INTRODUCTION

I feel at home in the mountains, wherever I am in the world. I am forever connected to my birthplace of Vermont by forests and steep hills, the gentle waves of the Green Mountains on the horizon.

Even in the desert, where the mountains take the form of vertical sandstone walls, I am comforted watching birds dip back and forth, dodging each other, gliding just feet from the ground, tilting their wings to cut turns, then flying back up towards the blue sky.

I feel a deep affection for the Canadian Rockies, where the mountains are sharp edifices of rock cutting through thick clouds; the erosion that shrunk the Green Mountains has not yet affected these peaks. In the summer, when the sky dims to dusk and thundering wind crashes through the valleys, I sleep deeply as my tent bends like a sail of a ship navigating through the granite seas.

I love hiking up to those alpine mountains, first walking through timberland, where branches wear lichen like wool, and then in the alpine, where the trees abruptly stop. Life that high—in the alpine—is harsh. The weather up there can easily take a life. There is little means for shelter or food. While I can't stay for long, it still feels like home.

January 11

6:45pm. I was alone in my apartment in Boston, sitting on my couch, focused on the glass of whiskey in front of me. It disappeared with one gulp. So smooth, warming, comfortable. It felt good, like an embrace. It felt like romance. It felt like everything I didn't have, everything I wanted. I couldn't get that kind of feeling without poisoning myself. I poured another glass.

This isn't healthy, I thought. But I couldn't stop. Somehow I ended up in a ditch, and the culmination of the previous six months had me digging deeper into it.

I graduated from a university in Boston a year prior. I had some okay friends there, but my passion didn't exist in that city. I was just stuck there, waiting for comfort to find me in a dark time. But I was being passive. I had to go out and find something more powerful than comfort; I needed a passion. Moreover, I needed the ability to create value for myself.

The past six months had been hard. At some point, I had convinced myself that I needed to prepare to settle down. I went through a few jobs, all of which I quit out of frustration. I felt stripped of my creative drive. They piled on monotonous busy work, and they cloaked my tasks in a mask of responsibility. But I never felt like I was being responsible. I was forcing myself to be a type of person I was not. I knew I needed to try something new, but a life reset is always overwhelming.

I think there's a tendency for recent university graduates to feel like they have just stepped into the *real world*, and whatever they are is what they will be forever, and if they don't love it, then tough luck. But aren't we always evolving as people? More importantly, don't we all have the power to create and change our own values as things change in life?

I recognize that asking these questions screams *privilege*. But the pressure I was feeling to live up to a higher standard was set by those with privilege to cast their standards onto others. Isn't it kind of bullshit to listen to that standard if it drives me to clutch a bottle of whiskey alone on a weekday?

This story is not about depression. The important thing, to me, is what happened afterward. I wish I could share this experience without starting from the pain I was feeling, but the unhappiness was what influenced the most important stage of my life.

My frustrations and failures were linked to many things going on. An ex girlfriend and I had just broken up, and we were both hurt in the process. I felt hopeless trying to find a job that I could see myself sticking with for the long-term. I lost all ability to control my anxiety. I began to think that my friends didn't believe in me. In my head, their words and interventions often sounded discouraging, but they were really just trying to catch me while I was falling. I didn't listen. I jumped right out of their arms. It didn't take long before I stopped believing in myself. That's when I started drinking way too much. Every little thing that didn't go right was adding up, and I felt like I had no avenues toward happiness. The worst of it all was the drinking. I was trying to numb my pain, but all the alcohol did was make it worse. A number of friends walked away from me at that time, and I have to admit that I understand their decisions to do so. I never want to be in that headspace again.

One particular source of happiness was obviously

missing from my life. I was avoiding my true love: the mountains. Climbing mountains is my passion, but, for some reason, *rock climber* didn't make it between businessman and engineer on the list of available jobs at my university's career fair. I suppose I took a break from the mountains with the hopes that I could pass off my love for climbing as just a hobby.

I'm a little envious of my friends who are so content in their *regular* jobs. It would make so many things—especially relationships with my family and friends—easier. But how could I keep myself from the mountains when they had always allowed me to feel my healthiest? After a few summers of road tripping and climbing some of North America's most beautiful peaks, the professional world held very little that could provide me with adequate stimulation. I began to wonder *why*. I knew I loved rock climbing, but why did it matter in the first place? What made the sport so important to me?

I reflected on that feeling of sore fingertips clinging to cold granite, balancing on rock features that narrowly allow for a hard-earned passage to a summit. At times, climbing can feel contrived. Often there is a hiking trail that goes around and to the top of some of the most incredible rock climbing routes, so why not just hike?

There's something special about looking for the

most aesthetic way to the top, about searching for a route that requires skill, perseverance, balance, and mental fortitude. My favorite climbs follow fluent crack systems that draw lines up steep, long faces, high in alpine environments on spires above icy, cracked glaciers. These places don't bear life well. Overcoming these unwelcoming places, or even attempting them only to turn around out of fear for danger, is an example of humankind's most powerful ability—to create value. I wanted to live a life guided by my own motivation.

So what did I really want? I loved writing and climbing. These two things were obsessions. They both require a creative process that I am deeply invested in. I wanted to combine those passions to create art, to tell stories. But first I had to figure out how I was going to make it work, and I was nervous about the risk involved in putting myself out there to share my art with others with no guarantee of praise or reward.

Some people in this world are incredibly intelligent artists and athletes, but those forms of intelligence seem to sit on the back burner behind more academic intelligences. If someone knows how to scale massive peaks, create music, dance, or make captivating photographs, why shouldn't those talents be viewed as a pathway toward success in the same way that being a natural mathematician is? More often than not, society undervalues these modes of creation as mere hobbies.

I lost track of time as I fell into my dream, but almost no time passed...It was still 6:45pm when I picked my phone off the coffee table, whiskey glass in the other hand, to answer a phone call. It was my closest friend, Zephyr, who was working as an engineer for a climbing gear company in Utah.

Zephyr and I had gone on the crown of all road trips a few years earlier. We drove from Boston to the north coast of Alaska, finding some of our favorite climbs of all time along the way. We went to university together, but we both spent more time climbing in New Hampshire than going to class. My excuse in the winter months usually had something to do with bad road conditions driving back to Boston from New Hampshire. Even though my apartment was right next to campus, one professor came to think I was commuting down to Boston every day and started wishing me a safe drive back to New Hampshire after class when I did manage to show up.

Zephyr is definitely more extroverted than me, but, together, we are always filled with energy. We're always planning big adventures, usually based around a potential first ascent. In climbing, a first ascent—a route that has never been done before—is a special achievement. It's something that goes down in history and can't be undone. While a speed record can be broken, a first ascent will always be just that—first. Our adventurous spirits were fueled by a quest for finding new routes up mountains. We consider ourselves artists in a way, working with the form of the world. Our climbs are marked by lines that we draw on our rocky canvases.

Zephyr had been on a climbing trip in Patagonia for the past couple of weeks and this call was the first I'd heard from him since he'd flown down there. I knew he was attempting an unclimbed tower with our mutual friend, Marc, so I was anxious to hear how it went.

"Zephyr! What's going on? How was Patagonia?" I was nervous he might notice that I was on the verge of slurring my words, but he was too quick to jump in to hear.

He replied in an excited and anxious tone, almost as if he was running for his life (which he actually had been not too long before). "Scary climb this trip. Shit rock. Worst I've ever hit. Legit scared." He wasn't even in Patagonia anymore, but there was still a sense of panic in his voice. He was unable to generate full sentences.

"Yikes. And we've climbed some brownie brittle," I replied, referring to the abundance of crumbly rock that we had overcome in the Rockies and Alaska on previous climbing trips.

"Yeah. It was wild. Base camp was 15 miles in over two glaciers. Way real."

"Damn." I took a sip of whiskey as I braced against my own wave of nervousness for my friend's safety.

"I'm glad you're still good. You're due for some Bugaboo granite right now."

The Bugaboos are an alpine climbing destination in the Purcell Mountains of British Columbia, a sea of glaciers with large granite spires protruding from the ice. Zephyr and I first visited the Bugaboos together a few years prior, and, since that trip, the Bugs had become my favorite climbing destination. Despite its alpine nature, the granite in the Bugs is of a high quality for climbing. Though there are some loose rocks, typical in the alpine, most of the climbing routes ascend really solid crack systems with secure holds. I consider it to be one of the most beautiful places in the world, hardly touched by human development, but still quite accessible for climbers willing to hike a few steep miles and cross snowy glaciers to approach long, gorgeous routes. It's certainly a commitment to go climbing in the Bugaboos, but it is nowhere near as demanding as Zephyr's undertaking in Patagonia.

"Oh, I need granite bad," Zephyr said with a pleading tone. "Something with an anchor besides two shit knifeblades. I plastered them as hard as I could."

Zephyr was referring to knifeblade pitons—thin pieces of metal, a few inches long, with a hole in the end to clip a carabiner to. Pitons were one of the earliest forms of climbing protection. They come in many shapes and sizes, but the knifeblades look just as their name implies. Pitons (also called pins) require a hammer to pound them into thin cracks in the rock. They can then be removed by hammering them back and forth and pulling sharply with a funkness (a metal cable that is clipped to a piton then yanked hard enough to shock load the pin out of a crack).

Modern climbing protection—most commonly, cams and nuts—is designed to be easily inserted and removed from cracks without a hammer, and, most importantly, they cause much less damage to the rock than pounding pitons. Nuts are simply chunks of metal attached to a cable that can be threaded into crack constrictions. However, cams have an active function. They have a set of lobes than can be contracted by a trigger that controls springs. When contracted, the cam is placed into a crack. It can hold a fall from its expanding force against the sides of the crack. When there are no cracks available to take removable protection, construction bolts are drilled into the rock.

Bolts leave a permanent trace, so good ethics require placing only as many bolts as are required for safety. Bolting equipment is also very heavy, and the hard-

wear is expensive, so it tends to be best to avoid bolts if possible. Nuts and cams usually won't fit in the extremely thin cracks that knifeblade pitons are made for. Thus, knifeblades are still useful on alpine routes with crumbly rock, where razor-thin cracks are often abundant.

I've been asked many times how climbers "get the ropes up there." The process of climbing tall mountains or cliffs usually involves two partners, a leader and a follower. The leader climbs up trailing a rope, which is tied to their harness. The rope runs through a belay device that the follower operates from below. As the leader climbs, they place removable metal protection in cracks and holes in the rock then clip their rope to the protection with carabiners. The further the leader climbs above their last piece of protection, the greater distance they would fall before the rope caught them if they were to slip.

Ideally, a leader will want to place protection frequently enough to prevent them from landing on the ground or a ledge if they were to fall. However, certain climbs may not have frequent enough cracks to accept the ideal amount of gear to protect against dangerous falls. In this case, the term "runout" is used. It is often indicated in guidebooks by the letter "R" following the name and grade of a climbing route. Runout climbs might sound foolish, and maybe they are, but Zephyr and I have found that the spiciness can add quite a bit of excitement and appeal.

Climbing ropes are measured using the metric system, and are usually 60 or 70 meters long. When the leader climbs to a point where they will soon run out of rope, they must build an anchor—usually with two or three pieces of protection—then belay the follower up so they can reset and start climbing again with the full length of rope available. Each reset is called a pitch. When the follower climbs, the rope is belayed from above, so that they will not fall more than a few inches (the length for a dynamic rope to stretch) if they fall. It's normal for experienced climbing partners to switch who is leading and who is following at each pitch, to split up the increased risk of taking a lead fall.

In North America, the difficulty of a rock climb is rated using the Yosemite Decimal System (YDS). The YDS has five classes to indicate the technical nature of the terrain. First class is walking on flat ground, second class is difficult hiking, third class is steep hiking that may require the occasional use of hands to clamber over rocks, and fourth class involves scrambling using hands and feet to climb over rocky terrain that is not quite vertical. Most climbers can physically handle fourth class terrain without a rope, but it can still get very exposed and dangerous, so protection is appreciated by many at that class.

Technical rock climbs fall into the fifth class. Ropes are usually used for fifth class climbing. In the YDS, *the 5 is followed by a decimal, which is followed by a number ranging from 1-15. This indicates how difficult the climbing moves are. To make it more complicated, any double digit rating is then broken down into four sub-ratings (a, b, c, d). As an example, 5.6 ends up being about as easy as the most basic climbs you would find at an indoor climbing gym. 5.8 is followed by 5.9, which is followed by 5.10a then 5.10b. The hardest climb completed to this day is 5.15d, which is so incredibly hard that I cannot fathom how it was possibly done. Ironically, the system matters little, because grades are given subjectively and are sometimes changed by consensus as more people climb the routes. Grades matter even less on big mountains where the technical rock climbing might not even be the hardest part of the whole expedition, given logistics, hazardous mountain terrain, and total distance traveled. Consequently, the climb Zephyr was attempting can't really be understood by a YDS climbing grade.*

Zephyr continued his saga. "We rappelled down a shooting gallery. Certain death if a rock came. Seven V-threads. Didn't hit the bottom until 11:30pm. Didn't get back to camp until 8am. We spent 30 hours out there."

V-threads are a type of anchor point used for rappelling down ice. They are created by drilling two intersecting holes with an ice screw so they create a V in the ice that the rope can be passed through. Drill-

ing V-threads can be time consuming, so rappelling seven times off V-threads down a gully with no other means for escape and an extreme hazard created by rocks potentially falling from above was definitely a dramatic undertaking.

"That's gnarly. Did you make it to the top?" I asked.

"Nope. 50-knot winds. Our rope was a sail up there. We hit the ridge at 9:30pm, then it would have been about three more hours of navigating more shit rock to get to the summit." He paused, and his tone turned from excitement to disappointment. "It's an unclimbed tower. Would have been sick and we almost had it."

Something about the phone call with Zephyr sparked a flame inside me again. As terrifying as that mountain sounded, I had to ask myself, *Why wasn't I there?*

I had spent years training and learning climbing skills so I could be out there with Zephyr, so that I could potentially do something meaningful for myself. I suddenly realized I was throwing all that away and accomplishing nothing else that I cared about.

I screwed the cap back on the whiskey, pulled out my laptop, and started planning for something new and exciting—a little life reset.

Breezy

I had wanted to adopt a dog for a while. I figured the companionship would be healthy, and I imagined adventuring across North America with a canine friend, road tripping, like in Steinbeck's *Travels with Charley.*

I had been casually browsing some dog adoption websites for a few months at that point. I remember being so nervous. Every time I found a dog I wanted to adopt, I would freak out a little and close out of the web page. How could I take care of another life when I could barely take care of my own? Eventually, I managed to convince myself that the responsibility would push me to buckle down and do what needed to be done for myself.

I found Breezy, a 15-pound terrier mix. She has tan and gray markings on her face, a black coat, blonde paws, and unmanageably wiry hair. Her profile on the shelter's website said she was about two years old and included a copy of a police report that revealed she was picked up as a stray outside of a gas station. Aside from that, her background was and still is a mystery.

Breezy was actually located in Houston, Texas when I adopted her, but there were so many dogs in need of homes down in that area that the shelter had posted her profile on an adoption site for Boston.

Two days after signing the paperwork, Breezy was on a flight to Boston, where I picked her up from the airport. I fell in love immediately when I took her out of her crate and held her for the first time. I don't care what anyone says. She's not just a pet. She's a daughter to me.

Breezy is quiet and mellow when it's time to hang out, but she's full of energy when it's time to adventure. She has no problem keeping up on long hikes, nor does she hesitate while scrambling over difficult rocky terrain. The best part, though, is that she loves riding in my backpack when I go on easy rock climbs. She's tough, a near-fearless 15 pounds.

In the beginning, her toughness especially came out around other dogs. She was like a gun firing whenever she saw a new dog. Another dog could be minding their own business on the other side of the street, but, if Breezy caught wind of them, I would have to be ready to manage Breezy's vicious barks. I kid you not, this micro-dog had the growl of a blood-thirsty wolf, quickly picking up the nickname *Wolfy*. But we worked on her social anxiety, and it didn't take long for her to start making a few canine friends.

Training Breezy turned out to be a hilariously frustrating endeavor. She is quite independent and very smart—too smart for her own good. She was quick to pick up commands, which also meant she was quick to learn how to piss me off. She loves to piss me off. That little punk does whatever she can to sneak off for a few hours and hunt rodents. From the start, she was incredibly skilled at slipping through my arms, finding open doors, and even chewing through her leashes. She'd eventually come back to me, covered in mud with a big grin on her face. She knew she would be in trouble, but she would always come right up to my feet then roll onto her back in hopes of a belly rub.

By mid-March, over a month after I adopted Breezy, I realized just how adventurous she was and felt confident we could hit the road together. I decided to build out a pickup truck to serve as our new home. I put a cap over the bed, built a platform for a twin-sized mattress with storage drawers underneath, and outfitted the roof with solar panels and batteries to power a mini-fridge, my laptop for writing, and fans to keep Breezy comfortable on warm days. It felt like the perfect way to live. I had everything I needed for life right there with me in the back of my truck at all times.

I called up Zephyr and couldn't hold in my excitement. "Breezy and I are coming west! See you in a couple days!"

"Hell yeah!" Zephyr exclaimed. "You're going to love this. I found a ton of unclimbed cliffs in the San Rafael Swell. Way out there in the desert."

"Time for us to get after it," I said. The next morning, I had my truck packed full of climbing gear, doggie toys, and everything I could need. Breezy and I were off to Utah.

Welcome to the Swell

I am often asked how I know whether or not something has been climbed before. The first step is to look at the records. Climbing ascents are surprisingly well-documented online and in public journals. Nevertheless, a number of climbs go undocumented, especially routes on unnamed formations in the Utah desert—where I would focus on developing new climbs for the next several months.

The biggest giveaway that a climbing route has never been ascended is the lack of any evidence that the rock feature was ever descended. If there's no existing way down, then it's likely that nobody has ever gone up. Unless there is a way to walk down (not common on the desert cliffs I was exploring), it is very hard to descend a cliff without leaving gear behind. Usually, first ascensionists will drill expansion bolts into the rock at the top of their route that they can rappel from. In other cases, there may be a big rock feature with some sort of leftover rope or webbing wrapped around it (called *tat*) that a rappel rope went through. If nothing was left behind for retreat, features on the rock are covered in dirt (a sign that nobody else has wiped away the slippery dust layers to get a better grip on the handholds), and there are loose rocks abound that weren't knocked down to clear a path up the route, then it's almost certain you're looking at a first ascent waiting to be established.

There are tons of climbers in the world, but few of them are actually dedicated to developing new climbing areas. It takes a lot of time to forge up an unknown path and a lot of money to leave behind bolted anchors for the descent. Few climbers think about the cost that goes into the established climbs they enjoy, even when they clip their rope into bolts that were obviously purchased and left behind by others for the pleasure and safety of future climbers.

Route development is a form of stewardship in the climbing community. It's also a form of art that is painted on the walls for the community to take pleasure in, to criticize freely, and to obsess over when a climb is so beautiful that people travel from all over the world to attempt it.

Route development has its own creative process. Learn the skills, get the equipment, find the rock— these are just part of the preparation. For me, the most exciting part is looking up at a wall from the ground, eyeing possible hand and foot holds, and comparing the size of cracks to your hand to determine what sizes of gear will be required. This is high-end connect-the-dots. There may be many ways to get to the top of a cliff, but the best ones follow the proudest lines. One option may appear to be the easiest way up with big ledges and blocks to clamber over. The climber with an artist's eye will often ignore those lines and look for the steepest, longest, most challenging way that follows a logical sequence of holds with the least amount of wandering back and forth. Flow is beauty. When you're climbing, a steady flow up vertical, clean, and challenging terrain feels good.

Then, when the line is picked, an attempt is made to climb it. Often the attempt is unsuccessful, sometimes due to hazards or a lack of gear or even the mental state of the climber. Turning around is always a fair decision when it's safe to do so, even if it's just because you're not feeling focused that day. You can always come back and try again.

Aside from the human mind and its potential for mistakes, the biggest danger in the desert is the rock. Climbing safety gear rarely fails, and, when it does, it is most likely due to misuse. But, in the desert, it is common to encounter *choss*—loose rock—ready to fall down and crush you if you so much as look at it funny. I would say it's best to avoid choss, but, truth be told, choss wrangling is a lot of fun. More often than not, first ascents would not be possible without taking on choss. By cleaning choss off the rock walls in a methodical manner, carefully tossing it off far away from your belayer, the route is made safer for future climbers.

The rock in the San Rafael Swell is no exception to the rule of choss. Actually, on many cliffs, the rock quality is worse than in most established climbing areas. I think Zephyr's perspective was altered by his experience in Patagonia. As we drove down dirt roads, more than an hour from the nearest pavement, Zephyr went off about how amazing this spot was going to be. I had climbed in the San Rafael Swell before, but *The Swell* encompasses an incredibly large area in the central Utah desert. This particular area in The Swell was a popular destination for rednecks kicking sand up on their ATVs, but it was relatively unexplored by climbers.

"Welcome to The Swell!" Zephyr shouted as the dirt road essentially hit a dead end, only further passable by overland vehicles.

I got out of my truck and looked around. The rock

sure was...something.

It was neither the bright red, crack split sandstone of Indian Creek nor the black varnished sandstone, begging to be climbed, of Red Rock in Las Vegas. It was a light-shaded sandstone. The cliffs could almost have been mistaken for towering sand dunes. I was immediately concerned that the rock wouldn't be strong enough to safely place protection in its cracks. A fall could easily generate enough force to blow the rock surrounding a cam to crumbles. But one thing was for sure: the area was gorgeous.

Birds were flying everywhere. The sandy walls had their own unique elegance, and the cliff line extended farther than I could see. At night, the stars appeared brighter than I could believe. I had thought I grew up with vibrant stars at my parent's home in Vermont, but there are no stars like those in the desert. The Swell was virtually free of light pollution, thus the visibility of outer space was expansive.

The rock might have been exceptionally chossy, but, after a day of poking around, I began to see Zephyr's vision for a new rock climbing area. The potential was there. Things just needed a little bit of sprucing up. Zephyr has always had an eye for these special places. First ascents aren't *gimmes*, and this rock was certainly not going to provide any gimmes. A lot of work had to be done to prep the routes for a first ascent, the slippery sand had to be dusted off the good holds and the choss had to be knocked out of the cracks.

There's something special and challenging about putting up a first ascent. It's like solving an unsolved puzzle. Imagine standing in a spot where nobody else has been. With Google Earth at our fingertips, it can seem like there are so few places on Earth that haven't been touched by humankind. But there's so much more exploring to do, especially in the vertical axis.

The art of the first ascent is connected to my creative drive. I get to build, develop, and design with my eyes, hands, and feet. It's a remarkable feeling—fingers running over the rock, searching for the next hand hold, finding the perfect spot to drill a bolt for protection on a sheer face so that it fits in with the climb and doesn't leave an unnecessary trace.

I couldn't stop smiling from just a few days into our work there. We had already established three new climbs. The sun roasted me all day, but I didn't mind one bit. With sand in my nose and laughter at Zephyr's loud banter, I hadn't been that happy in a long time.

Perhaps Breezy loved it there the most. She pranced through the sand after the many new smells, and, while we climbed, she sat and watched curiously, occasionally breaking her focus to dig a hole.

At night, the temperature dropped and Breezy would snuggle up under the blankets. She wasn't much of a cuddler at first, but she warmed up to it. Eventually, she became so comfortable sleeping in the bed of my truck that the place turned into her own little castle. I didn't mind that she would push me to the very edge of the mattress, at least until she woke me in the morning by walking on my face.

Every morning, we woke up in The Swell to the sun shining. We took our time. We ate slow breakfasts, enjoyed big cups of coffee, jogged around with Breezy, and told the same jokes over and over again, but we were always packed up and ready to climb by 9am. There have been many times in my life when I was lucky if I didn't have to force myself out of bed, rush to work, then barely start anything productive by 9:30. I think my pleasant, relaxing mornings in The Swell were a testament to my happiness there.

It wasn't all perfect though. There was one thing from my recent past that I hadn't left behind when I went west to pursue my new identity, and that was alcohol. In the desert, Zephyr and I would crack open beers every night. After a couple beers, I'd pour myself a cup of whiskey.

I thought back to my first real drink. I was in high school. It was one shot of gin, and that's all I had that night. Once I started college, I was rarely able to have just one drink. One drink always turned to two, which turned to six, which would turn to me just pulling straight from a bottle of booze. By my senior year of college, I made a habit of drinking every day of the week. A number of friends tried to talk me into laying off the whiskey. I even tried to quit a few times, but I would always cave after a few days off. *It's only one drink. This time I'll be able to consume in moderation.* I fooled myself every time.

Alcohol has been an unhealthy crutch for me through many sad times. It felt like it had pain-numbing effects, but it ultimately kept me tied to my sadness. It prevented me from overcoming depression, it locked me inside of it.

I reflected on a few too crazy nights fueled by booze while I drank under those desert stars. I felt queasy as I remembered all the nights that I'd spent puking my brains out. It must have been a few dozen. I thought about the night I woke up in my friend's arms in a bathroom stall after I had passed out while dancing on stage at a club. Damn, I loved to dance when I was drunk.

I remembered the hole I burned through my shirt with a cigarette on New Year's Eve that year. I re-membered the angry drunk texts I sent that night to everyone I had a falling out with. Nobody deserved what I said. I deeply regret how I directed my pain. I was broken-hearted and intoxicated, but those were two piss-poor excuses.

I didn't listen, and that was the problem. I didn't listen to my friends, so some gave up on trying to help me. I didn't listen to myself when I knew I was doing things wrong, so I kept making the same mistakes.

My issue was that, despite my attachment to booze, I was not the person I wanted to be when I was drunk. I saw how my habit turned away friends, how my resulting anger and blind actions hurt people I cared about, how unhealthy I was when I was under the influence. But there was something about that warm, sweet taste of booze that I couldn't easily walk away from. That addiction kept me tied to the parts of my past that I was not happy with.

I finished my cup of whiskey. It hit the knot I felt in my stomach—the anxiety induced from my introspection. I called it a night.

Zephyr and I started exploring some canyon systems between the rock walls, hoping to find access to more hidden cliffs with climbing potential. We scrambled up dusty gullies, pushed through prickly bushes, and skirted around stagnant pools trapped in depressions along the canyon floor—habitats for the forgotten plants that call such an ecosystem home.

At one point, we hit a dead end in the canyon maze, but we decided to continue upward. Zephyr led a pitch up a steep, blank slab. There were no obvious holds, just the friction of his climbing shoes and hands against little grooves in the rock surface. Soon after he climbed out of sight, the rope stopped moving, and, after a minute, he was ready to belay me up the pitch.

"Alright, Ari. This will be the best anchor you'll ever climb on," Zephyr yelled down to me.

I started climbing up and responded, "Is that sarcasm?"

"How much do you weigh?" he asked.

I'm a pretty light guy. "130 soaking wet."

Zephyr laughed and said, "Should be fine, just don't fall."

I won't even tell you what that anchor was, but let's just say my life wasn't going to be saved by much. It's not like Zephyr didn't know how to build safe anchors. That was classic Swell climbing. There just weren't any safe places to put protection into the crumbly rock. That's one of the reasons climbing there is such a challenge and adventure.

We kept climbing on easier terrain until we were only one pitch from the rim. It was my lead, so I climbed off our single-piton belay and led the entire pitch without placing any other gear for protection. I didn't really have any options. Fortunately, the climbing was well within my ability, so I was confident that I would not fall.

That particular formation didn't have many cracks for cams and nuts. We had to get creative on our way down since we didn't have any bolts to leave behind for rappel anchors. For one rappel, we jammed a bunch of sticks into a crack and slung our rope around it. It was actually pretty decent... for dead sticks, that is. What wasn't decent was the anchor we made by stacking a bunch of rocks on top of each other. Zephyr weighted it and the anchor started sliding, so we just stacked more rocks on top until it became fairly decent.

Maybe this makes us sound stupid, but I believe it was a testament to our skillful creativity. I know very few climbers who would've been able to rappel off that route as quickly as Zephyr and I did. Altogether, we rappelled five pitches of uncharted, nearly featureless terrain and left behind no metal gear, finding unique solutions in the environment around us. The mission proved our escape competency, which is essential for anyone who wants to climb at a high level and live to tell about it.

The lacking protection was indeed frightening, even though I knew the risk of deadly error was very low. Consequences make things exciting, but it's risk that makes things scary. That's when adventure is optimal—when the consequences and perceived risk are high but the objective risk is low.

My favorite route I established in The Swell at that time was a 5.10b sport climb that I named *Breezy's Palace. Sport* just means that the climbing is protected solely by bolts, because there are no cracks to make removable protection possible. I think bolting a climb is justified when a route is just so beautiful that it begs you to climb it. Regardless of the route, since bolts are permanent alterations to the cliff, it's always important to me that the bolts are placed minimally—only as many as needed to keep the climber safe.

Zephyr dragged me through some horribly prickly bushes into an alcove hidden among the cliffs. "Check out this wall. The little crimps and edges are all there. I think it could go as a sport climb."

The route was in a pretty spectacular spot. This alcove had a sandy base with giant walls surrounding its nearly circular floor. It felt like I was standing at the bottom of a silo with an open roof. The sandstone was grayish, with stripes of red and tan. Breezy made herself right at home in the alcove, digging holes in the sand, patiently waiting for Zephyr and me to climb.

Two ways exist to bolt a sport route. For particularly difficult climbs, it may be necessary to hike around to the top, rappel down, and drill the bolts before the route has actually been climbed. If it's the only way to make a new 5.15d possible, then I understand. That kind of climb is too cutting edge to bolt while simultaneously climbing the route. On a personal level, I am not a fan of this style. It feels like the adventure is stripped from the process of route development. I set a standard for myself that, if I was going to bolt this sport climb, it would need to be done ground up, on lead.

The first few moves on the climb are slabby. The angle of the rock starts off slightly less than vertical on really thin edges. It was a gentle balancing act. A lot of the weak holds would break off under body weight, since nobody had climbed the route before.

Zephyr started up the route first, meticulously tapping every hold with his hands to test the rock's integrity before fully committing to a move. He climbed up to a comfortable resting position, then pulled up the drill on a thin rope that he tagged behind him so he wouldn't have to climb with all of the heavy bolting equipment dangling from his harness. It was a relief when the first bolt went in, since it was now the only protection between Zephyr and the ground.

He made a few more moves, got the next bolt in, then looked up with uncertainty. The route began to steepen and there seemed to be a blank section between Zephyr and an obvious hold above. Zephyr clipped himself directly to the bolt and leaned back to take a break. "Want to give this next section a try?" he asked me.

I lowered Zephyr, tied into the rope, and climbed up to where he left off. I had to spend a few minutes hanging around before I found a sequence that looked good. It's definitely an unsettling feeling, looking around for potential holds, moving upwards while knowing your next bolt doesn't even exist yet. In that position, climbs that aren't necessarily hard can suddenly feel far out of reach. I had doubts about every move I made.

I pulled the next few moves through the steep section on small holds, then reached for a big hold where I could take a rest and drill in the next bolt. From there, the next few moves would be the crux of the climb, the hardest section. I had to pull hard on the edge of a big hold with my left hand and jump ever so slightly off my toes to grab another good hold with my right hand. Then, I had to kick my right foot out onto a blank slab to my side and use friction to reposition myself for the next sequence. One more bolt, a long rest, then a mantle onto a ledge ended the hardest section. That ledge had a lot of loose rock on top, so I had to spend some time pulling off fragile holds before I climbed the last bit of easy slab to a ledge where I drilled two bolts for an anchor.

I loved that route because it flowed so well up the center of such an aesthetically-pleasing wall. I took a moment to think about what I had created. I no longer felt like I was floundering, like I had when I was in Boston. For the most part, I felt like I was doing what made me whole.

Remember when I said that route development was stewardship for the climbing community? Well, it doesn't always start off like that. Until new routes are shared with the world, they are often cloaked in secrecy. This isn't the case when new routes are developed in already popular climbing areas, but when a new wall is established in an area that doesn't see much climber traffic, it is often spoken about in hushed tones, shared only with the developer's closest friends.

Not every climber agrees with this kind of secrecy, but an argument can be made that it is fair for a developer to want to cherry-pick the best first ascents before word gets out about a new area with route potential. Climbing ethics tend to respect this entitlement. I abide by that rule, though I must admit that I am critical of the sentiment involved. It feels rather colonialist to lay claim to an area like that. I may be labeled a hypocrite, but I don't entirely think this sort of claim is moral despite my actions as a first ascensionist. In climbing, the idea of conquering mountains is nearly universal. I never liked the term conquering. It's apparent how inappropriate that attitude is in a place like the San Rafael Swell. Many of the sandstone walls in the Swell display incredibly well-preserved indigenous petroglyphs that serve as a reminder of those who were there first. My first ascents tell a part of my story, but that does not make those walls mine. I think it's important for climbers to act intentionally on the land they use, to appreciate it and create art with it, but not to conquer it.

Climbing philosophy is far from perfect. I want to influence a more intentional philosophy in the climbing community, but I do not always know how. One problem with climbing is that it's a sport for doers, but us climbers don't always think about why we do the things we do. Why do we climb? The Swell got me thinking about this. I wanted to know if there was any justice to the sport.

There is a lot of gray area when it comes to philosophizing about outdoor recreation. Many are divided by the circulation of information about new climbing areas. More people in an area can bring growth to a nearby struggling economy, and more accessible climbing areas allow more people to enjoy the sport. But once a wall ends up in the public domain, the developer loses control of the art that is created there.

The area is opened up to more traffic, which could arguably be detrimental to the land. I struggle to decide what's more important: accessibility or preservation in the outdoors.

Many people and organizations have trouble balancing this, including the National Park Service. Edward Abbey's writings enhance this conflict. I want everyone to be able to experience the outdoors as I do—to benefit from the health that it provides. But then I imagine The Swell undergoing the kind of development Arches National Monument was subjected to, recorded by Abbey in his book Desert Solitaire, as roads and facilities were built and more tourists started to visit.

Abbey proposed that we eliminate cars in national parks by building parking lots outside and requiring tourists to hike in. He likens national parks to holy places, reasoning that one wouldn't drive a car into a church. I think it's fair to say that the parks are for the people, not for their motors, but is it reasonable to expect that the people could possibly access and enjoy the beauty of the parks without their cars? Abbey believes that millions of Americans, especially the young, yearn for challenge and adventure. I'm not convinced that only adventurous and capable people should have the right to see national parks in person. Who are we to say how and why others get to access the outdoors?

The desert is a special place. Its sandstone towers provoke wonder. It's hard to not look at them in awe. How could these fragile skyscrapers so naturally protrude from this seemingly barren landscape? But it is far from barren. What it lacks in trees it far makes up for in microscopic marvels of life. Cryptobiotic crust, layers of living organisms hidden in the soil, are precious habitats that can easily be crushed by human footsteps. Even the tiniest of cacti, Breezy's biggest nemeses, try to defend the landscape with their formidable needles.

We are capable of destroying all of it with roads and buildings and trails and masses of people bringing harm to the environment. Even I alone pose an impact by tromping on the earth, drilling bolts in the rock, pulling fragile features off the cliffs to suit my own selfish sport. I certainly feel guilty because of this. I want to believe that the climbing is worth the impact. Sometimes I justify my actions because I am only one person. But when one person comes, hundreds often follow. Just imagine what harm hundreds of visitors each day could do to the landscape. At least roads keep visitors on one path, hopefully preserving the surroundings. But perhaps these wild places are depreciated by human-built machines. How much impact is too much? I do not know where the line is.

Zephyr had to go back to work, so it was time for me to find another worthy climbing partner to share The Swell with. When I heard that my friend

Kelsey was nearby on a climbing trip in Indian Creek, I immediately called her up to show her the desert paradise that I had been living in. I had met Kelsey a year before on a climbing trip in Squamish, British Columbia. We immediately bonded, sharing our fondness for climbing offwidth cracks (cracks bigger than the size of your fist, so climbing them requires a lot of squirming and jamming full body parts into the cracks). Offwidth climbing is a constant battle, sometimes a bloody game. I often joke that a gear list for offwidth requires whiskey and gauze. Fun certainly isn't a word I'd use to describe it, but Kelsey was addicted to this practice of overcoming the terrible.

There were many offwidths that I had picked out, most far too difficult for me. But when Kelsey first arrived in The Swell, she was as skeptical as I was at first. She hadn't climbed on chossy rock before, and she was hesitant to try any of the routes I had saved for her. Nevertheless, I knew Kelsey could find the headspace to overcome the choss. It only seemed logical that an offwidth climber could prevail over any kind of discomfort.

Kelsey, a biologist by profession, quickly fell in love with the environment there—especially the birds. She had recently been involved in a research study that sparked her interest in birding, and there were so many different types of birds in The Swell, even a few that Kelsey had never seen before. We walked along battered ATV paths with Breezy, watching the birds fly around us. The funny thing is that I hadn't really noticed the variety of birds before Kelsey got there. All I had to do was shift my focus away from the rock to open my eyes to the rest of the wonders around me.

Eventually Kelsey decided to try a crack on a brilliant formation that jutted out like a big prow from the cliff band. She started up the first few easy moves, pulling blocks out of the crack to clear her path. As she moved higher, I could see her legs start to tremble. She hesitated. I could hear doubt in her voice as she quietly talked herself through the next move. It wasn't physically hard, but I could see why it was scary. The next move would require her to step out onto a big block of questionable integrity. I moved to belay her from the side of the route, so any rockfall would hopefully avoid me. She took a deep breath and moved on, legs still trembling, and succeeded in pulling herself onto a big ledge where she would place the anchor.

Kitty Gnar Gnar! Kelsey named the route. I followed up the climb and gave her a big hug at the top. She had a huge smile on her face. Not only was this her first time climbing a first ascent, but she was also incredibly proud for venturing out of her comfort zone by climbing on uncertain rock. That kind of pride is the driving factor behind Kelsey's attraction to challenge, and I really admire her for it.

Later that night, we were cooking dinner at camp when she said to me casually, "You know, I've realized that choss really isn't a big deal at all. You just have to be a little more careful, go around it, or clean it off."

"Now you get it," I said and smiled. "Welcome to The Swell."

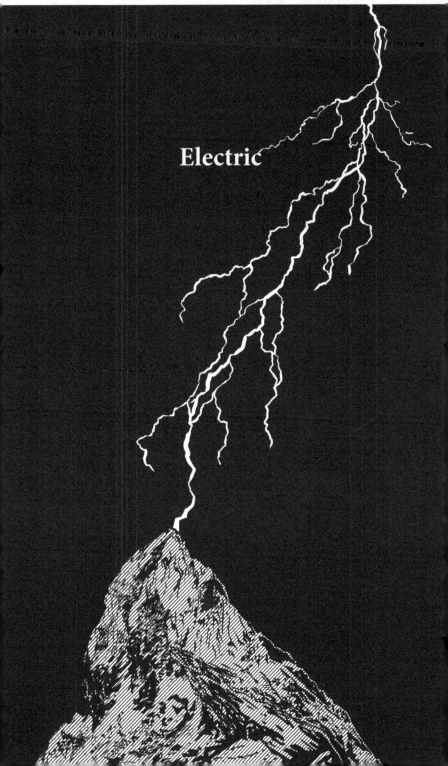

Electric

The desert was starting to get too hot to climb with summer coming, so I decided to head north to the place that has inspired me the most: Bugaboo Provincial Park in British Columbia, Canada.

Unfortunately, I couldn't bring Breezy into the Bugaboos. Not only are dogs not allowed in the park, but it also wouldn't have been a safe environment for her. Inconsistent weather, high elevation, and long routes make the danger of climbing in the *Bugs* far beyond the hazards of the desert.

So far, I hadn't spent a day without Breezy. The thought of her staying with a sitter for a week made me nervous, but I figured it would be good for her to get a little break from me. I had to convince myself that it wasn't a big deal. Deep down, I felt sad leaving her, and I knew nights would be lonely without her sleeping by my side.

The Bugaboos are pretty much the opposite of the San Rafael Swell, but I was so excited for the change of seasons, to trade sandstone desert climbing for granite alpine climbing. The desert has a dry, sandy feel. The sun shines on you and it's easy to smile. The alpine air feels cold, even on sunny days. The granite feels sharp on your fingertips. The mountains are giants that look down at you with an intense stare. They let you know they are in charge. My heart flutters when I look up at those mountains.

Alpine environments are where I thrive. They are why I fell in love with climbing. The Bugaboos, in particular, are a magical alpine playground. High in the mountains of eastern British Columbia, tall granite spires and beautiful snowy glaciers call my name. I dream of that place all year, waiting for the short summer climbing season when the conditions in the Bugaboos are best. But, even though summer brings better weather to the Bugs, the weather is still volatile. Storms can be on the forecast almost every day, and a prominent spire is the last place you want to be during a storm. On the flip side, those elements out of your control add to the challenge of alpine climbing and make the successful ascents that much more rewarding.

Even just getting into the Bugaboos requires a steep hike carrying lots of gear to make a base camp below the actual climbs. Then, some objectives up there take full or even multiple days filled with constant climbing before returning to camp. It's not a holiday. Alpine climbing beats you up. The funny thing is, a trip to the Bugaboos might sound like a vacation, but the alpine is where I work my hardest.

My friend Liz joined me on this trip to the Bugs. Liz and I had gone to the same university, but we hadn't started climbing together until after we graduated. Liz lived in Seattle, working as a geologist, and I had struck up a friendship with her while bumming on her couch during a climbing trip in the Cascade Mountains the previous summer.

Liz is fairly quiet, but bold. Her smile is inviting, and her motivation in the mountains is fierce. She's an awesome climbing partner. She is ready to take on challenges, but she's smart, never reckless. There's a difference between bailing to avoid environmental dangers and giving up because a climb feels scary. Often, in life, fear indicates danger. But fear in the mountains just keeps climbers in check. It keeps us on our toes. Sometimes, when I get scared—perhaps due to insecure holds, high exposure, or just a weird mental space—I freeze up, and a move that I am physically able to do without falling can suddenly feel impossible. Overcoming fear is just a part of the challenge. I've never seen Liz back down from a scary climbing move. There are very few people who can take a deep breath, push through moments of uncertainty, and come back hungry for more each time like she does.

Liz and I decided to climb the Northeast Ridge of Bugaboo Spire—the namesake mountain in the park. Looming high above the Applebee Campground, where Liz and I made camp, Bugaboo Spire is dark, rugged, and gorgeous. Its stunning appearance lures in climbers, and the best way to the top, in my opinion, is up the Northeast Ridge.

Bugaboo Spire was first climbed by Conrad Kain in 1916 up the South Ridge, now called the *Kain Route*. Kain, an Austrian climbing guide who became the Alpine Club of Canada's first professional guide, is revered in the mountaineering community for his nearly 70 first ascents in Canada.

At the time, the Kain Route was groundbreaking. I could hardly imagine leading the crux with the equipment Kain would've had at the time—hemp rope tied around the waist, hobnail boots, and no fall protection. The crux of the Kain Route is beautiful, navigating a giant rock pillar—the *gendarme*—up an exposed, delicate slab.

Despite the historically significant and exciting

crux, I don't find the entirety of the Kain Route to be very aesthetic by modern alpine climbing standards. The majority of it is gravelly, third-class hiking and scrambling up a wandering ridge. It's especially easy to get lost on the descent. Many parties have found themselves in trouble by veering too far off of the ridge proper. When I first climbed the Kain Route, I ended up only slightly off route on the descent and was forced to make a terrifying rappel down a rockfall-prone gully, then had to traverse exposed choss to get back on track.

Though we wouldn't be going up the Kain Route this time, Liz and I would be descending it, as it's the best descent off Bugaboo Spire, requiring a few rappels and a lot of downclimbing on easy terrain. Part of what makes the Northeast Ridge such a big undertaking is that long pass over. Not only would we have to climb twelve pitches of beautiful 5.8 granite cracks, but then we'd need to scramble traverse across the summit of Bugaboo Spire in order to descend the entire Kain Route. It's a full day, but well worth the effort.

The Northeast Ridge was first climbed in 1958 by Dave Craft, David Isles, Richard Sykes, and John Turner. It gained popularity after its inclusion in Steve Roper and Allen Steck's book *Fifty Classic Climbs of North America*, first published in 1979. Not only was this an iconic climbing guidebook, but it was also a captivating history of some of the most interesting climbs in America. The book may be the most classic piece of climbing literature to date, thus earning the nickname *Fifty Crowded Climbs* due to the influence it has had on the popularity of many included routes.

Despite the popularity, Liz and I only encountered two other parties on the route that day, and we all stayed far out of each other's way. The gorgeous climbing and the astounding views were ours to enjoy in near silence.

We left camp before sunrise and hiked across the Crescent Glacier to the bottom of a steep but short pitch, which we free-soloed, meaning that we climbed without a rope or any protection, up to the col below the start of the Northeast Ridge. We traversed across the snowy col and up to the start of the steep section, where we roped up for the first pitch of vertical climbing.

The best part of the climb was the view to the north. We looked out toward the remote Vowell Mountains and beyond. I've always loved looking out that way. It's a seemingly endless view of snow-capped peaks and bold granite towers, with glaciers winding between them.

Liz and I made fairly quick work of the Northeast Ridge, but, even as we topped out on the last pitch, our day was far from over. We still had a lot of scrambling over airy terrain to make it over the summit of Bugaboo Spire. Unbeknownst to us, bad weather had been moving in from the south, and, as we neared the summit, we could finally see what had been blocked by the mountain all day—storm clouds moving quickly toward us. We weren't the first people to get in trouble like that. Even the guidebook for the Bugaboos warns that many poor endings start with clear skies and perfect weather. Unexpected storms should be expected up there, and it's not uncommon for them to sneak up from out of sight. We didn't luck out that day.

We did what we could to pick up the pace, but our movement began to feel agonizingly slow with trouble coming soon. We were simul-climbing, which meant we had no anchor or standard belay. Instead, we were both tied into the rope, climbing at the same time while I placed protection at the lead and Liz cleaned it while she followed. At times, we had only one piece of protection between us, which was pretty nerve-racking. Imagine one person slipping, pulling the other person off with them, then having two people dangling from just one piece. But we had to stay confident in the other's ability to climb without falling. And, while the rest of the way up and over the summit was fairly easy, the stakes were high, the wind was picking up, and my nerves were starting to go wild.

I reached the first bolted rappel anchor, clipped

into it, then started to give Liz a regular belay. I could see her struggling to get her footing on a traversing, snow-covered slab as she gripped a little finger-sized crack in the rock to keep herself from sliding.

"We have to go!" I yelled.

I hated to feel like I was pressuring her to move faster than she could, but we really needed to get off that mountain, and we still had a long, dangerous descent ahead of us. Then, suddenly, it came. The thunder broke through the dark clouds looming above us with a crack. I felt like the sky struck a whip down onto me. I flinched, Liz and I locked eyes, and we could see each other's fear. Liz pushed her tangled red hair out of her face and thrashed her way over to me.

We got down the first rappel and started scrambling across third-class terrain toward the next rappel station. Then the rain started. It came quickly, harshly, and soaked everything around us. We crawled over rocks, our feet slipping, desperate for traction. Then the rain stopped suddenly. Everything was quiet for a moment.

Could it all be over? I thought, but too soon.

Thunder cracked again, this time louder. We kept moving, another rappel, then more third-class along a narrow catwalk. My heart was racing, my fingers trembling. At this point, Liz and I were no longer using the climbing rope to save as much time as possible. We had to keep moving fast, but we also had to be careful not to fall off the slender ridge, or else we'd plummet over a thousand feet to our deaths.

I could see the next bolted rappel anchor. It was only about 20 feet away, but then I noticed something—a sound, a buzzing. It made me pause. I looked down at the metal climbing gear attached to my harness and could see it vibrating. *Shit.* The buzzing sound got louder, unlike anything I had ever heard before. Imagine the music to a horror film, crescendoing right before a character opens a door that really shouldn't be opened.

Our elevation was over 10,000 feet, and we were right in the storm, exposed on a prominent mountain with nothing to protect us from the electricity. We were screwed. I frantically starting pulling the gear off my harness, tossing carabiners and cams, several of them tumbling off the ridge, never to be seen again. Then I saw a flash. For a millisecond, everything went white. I felt a shock run up my spine then circumnavigate my head. It was like electricity was conducting along the sweat line where my helmet met my forehead. I yelled in pain. I looked back at Liz, and I'm sure she saw a look on my face that expressed exactly what I felt—*we were going to die.*

The buzzing stopped, then came back again, distinctly conducting up the tapered ridgeline towards me. I felt another shock, and my vision went blurry for a second. This one was far less painful, but, fueled by fear, I yelled just as loud as the first time. I turned back to check on Liz and realized she had both of our ice axes strapped to her pack, sticking up like two lightning rods on her back. "Ditch the ice axes!" I yelled at her. She immediately pulled her pack off and stuffed the two axes into a crack at her feet.

My head was throbbing by the time we reached the next rappel station. I imagined lightning hitting the metal bolts, conducting down the wet rope, right to the metal belay device attached to my crotch while rappelling down. But we had no choice. Our position was far too exposed to sit this storm out.

As the terrain eased out going down to more manageable (but still wet) downclimbing, we began to calm ourselves. The buzzing had settled for the time being, and, when we started to hear that horrible sound running up the ridge, we were able to get off the most exposed sections to lay low and wait for it to stop. Still, we were cold, shaken up, and tired. We just wanted to be in our sleeping bags, but we still had to cover a bit of terrain to get down the Kain Route, then rappel three times down a steep snow slope to get off the col, and finally hike across the

Crescent Glacier back to camp.

I snapped a picture of Liz toward the bottom of the descent thinking I could share it and hopefully laugh about the situation once it was all over. I never ended up sharing it, though, because the expression on her face was just too real. It was full of pain, terror, exhaustion, and every emotion between.

The storm finally settled as we reached the glacier below. We walked back toward camp in silence. I couldn't believe how good we had felt climbing up the Northeast Ridge only a few hours before. It was such an amazing route, but it was so hard to remember what *amazing* could have felt like. I thought to myself, *How can I love being in the mountains so much when they could do this to me—or they could do even worse? Are the moments of joy worth the risk?*

These questions often feel impossible to answer.

Climbing can be hard to understand, because its results are often intangible. The reason why anyone would climb is often so hard to describe, but it holds a certain sentiment and spirit to many that answers why without words.

How can climbing be worthwhile if it gives nothing tangible to the world? It is hard to reason that a summit could possibly be an achievement worth dying for.

Reason and passion often collide in a harsh civil war within ourselves. But they can work together, and they do for the best climbers. Reason, without passion, keeps one grounded in the valleys where they can't see beyond the claustrophobic mountainsides. Passion, without the support of reason, threatens a climber with fatal falls. This is what risk management looks like in the mountains. Still, I often doubt climbing's value. I may feel like I love it, but am I just being foolish with my time? Death is a consequence up there. Am I actually willing to die for a mountain? I would need some time to really process these questions.

Liz and I finally made it back to camp, but something wasn't right. I couldn't find our tent anywhere. I stood right where I thought we had set it up, but it wasn't there. Then I noticed that the anchor lines I had tied to the rocks around the tent were still on the ground. The tent wasn't attached to them anymore. I looked around and caught a glimpse of something bright and orange, wrapped around a metal post with hooks that campers use to hang up their backpacks out of reach from critters.

Wait, is that…

It was my tent—ripped to shreds, poles broken, tied down to the post with all of our soaked sleeping gear stashed inside.

A man's head poked out of a nearby tent. "Sorry about your tent," he said. "It got crazy windy down here. We were able to catch it before it blew too far, and did our best to salvage your gear."

I was speechless. I couldn't believe we had no tent to crawl into after climbing through that storm. I was grateful that some friendly bystanders had been able to save my sleeping bag, sleeping pad, and camera. Nevertheless, my motivation was crushed. Liz and I were over it. We called the climbing trip short and hiked out.

On the way down, we passed a marmot with a tan and gray face looking right at us. It reminded me of Breezy, and all I wanted was to be with her again in the comfort of a home.

I called Zephyr as soon as I got cell phone service again to tell him about the trip. "Why do we like climbing?" I asked. "There's so much danger and discomfort. I know I love the mountains, I know I'll go back up there, but I want to know *why* it's worth it."

"I think the discomfort is why I love it," Zephyr said. "I don't know, I'm just so attracted to the idea of going through hell to achieve something." For Zephyr, it doesn't matter that the summits are meaningless when he has to dig deep down inside himself to reach them. The value is in the discomfort and the risk, not the summit.

I wondered for a moment if it was akin to asceticism, if the discomfort was a form of self-discipline. I was unsure. The thing with asceticism is that it's usually a means to an end, to an afterlife. Nevertheless, without purpose, the end is really just death. There are two ways to look at climbing: as a means to the summit or as a process. In my opinion, at the end of life, the value isn't in death; it's in the whole life that was lived.

Some say climbers have the shortest memories. Perhaps that is why so many climbers go back to the places that almost kill them. I don't want to romanticize danger and pain, but I cannot help but feel such a passion for it. The mountains pull me back every time, and I don't know exactly why.

My Temple

I've heard people refer to climbing as their religion and the mountains as their temples.

In the past, I've advocated against the published spiritualization of the wilderness and the likening of mountains to cathedrals. Often, when people deify outdoor spaces, they do not consider how much of a privilege it is to find spirituality in the outdoors.

I've feared that glorifying particular wild places could make the outdoors even more inaccessible. It is hard enough for most people to get involved with outdoor recreation in the first place. Equipment and travel alone are incredibly expensive, and it's not easy to learn how to recreate without a like-minded outdoor community to get involved with. By spiritualizing certain outdoor places and putting the freedom to explore on a pedestal, the accessibility of the outdoors is reduced further. I don't think going outside should require traveling to the most majestic places. Without a doubt, certain natural places inspire me more than others, but my perspectives are based on what I see. I don't want to imply that the places I love are more valuable than alternate places that different people may love for their own reasons. For some, a park in the city or a treehouse in a yard is good for some outdoor fun. I don't want to isolate people who can't explore the many places to which I have been fortunate enough to travel. It's a tough line to walk as a writer. Beautiful words have power to add embellishment to the world, but I truly believe there is much to be discovered right outside everyone's door. All it takes is an adventurous motive.

This perspective was shaped by some volunteer work I did to bring a diverse group of high schoolers on day hikes in the Middlesex Fells Reservation about six miles from downtown Boston. A lot of those kids needed a way to get out of the house on weekends. Their connection to the environment was built through recreation and community. I never imagined talking about a spiritual connection to the land with those kids. I don't think many of them would have been interested in that. However, I was recently connected to a citizen of the Nüümü and Yokut Nations, who broadened my view of using religion and spirituality to help underrepresented kids access the outdoors. She has done tremendous work to connect indigenous youths to their homelands through climbing and hiking, often using spirituality to make these kids aware of their inherent connection to the land. They even start climbing trips off with a prayer. She made it clear that all land is sacred to someone, and that sacred connection is one way to make the outdoors more accessible.

Everyone experiences the outdoors in their own way. The holy perspective of nature that is often portrayed in popular media requires a certain advantage to experience. It is not possible for everyone to stand on top of Yosemite's Cathedral Peak in order to get close to God. That kind of imagery can be isolating for those who do not or cannot feel it. On the other hand, I've learned that spiritual imagery can also be empowering for those with the background to connect with it. I cannot say that I have ever had something that I've worshipped, but I feel open to exploring this kind of deification some more—to entertain some experiential debate, to hopefully understand my personal purpose. I wonder, particularly considering the application of asceticism, in what ways climbing is like religion.

The value of life has changed greatly over the millennia. Religion once played a much larger role in understanding value. God's history of creation helped society understand morality in a world so complex that it required simplification—the moral codes of religion. Atheism may be much more common today than it was a thousand years ago, but similar moral codes have continued on, even for those who don't believe in God.

I've found that very few people ask *why* society became a certain way, while many people assume the way things are now is natural. By society's majority standards, mountain climbing is not fun. Rather, it's a masochistic sport and it is certainly not seen as valuable. But what gives anything else more value?

Certain religions have asked humanity to give up many sources of pleasure and function as a path to the afterlife. Does religion, with its rules and restrictions, create self-inflicted restraint? What is the point? Does religion create pain, which in turn creates form and meaning? Perhaps self-inflicted restraint is a way of demonstrating power. Maybe the pain felt while climbing is similar.

Why do people embrace asceticism? What does self-discipline help us achieve? It fills a need for a goal. Truth must be sought; it won't present itself on its own. Asceticism, in religion, is used as a tactic for gaining access to knowledge. Could the self-discipline required to overcome difficult goals in climbing similarly create form for life?

Asceticism is not inherently good, but it can be good as the means to a good end if it is used to enhance human energy to create value for life. However, asceticism can be dangerous. It can deprive the will of the mind if ascetic actions are not intentional. In that case, the only end goal is death.

Asceticism is dangerous when people expect intellect to come hand in hand with it. I see this as a passive approach. This kind of ascetic form relies on the truth coming forward by denying will. I'd much rather go after truth. I don't believe truth will come to me on its own. Knowledge is reliant on a broad range of perspectives. Imagine the vastness of human perspective. Everyone views things in different ways. So many differing messages can be drawn from art, nature, joy, and life. Thus, despite wanting to understand truth, I cannot believe there is such a thing as an objective understanding. Asceticism, as a way of life, is not a path to truth. Nor is mountain climbing.

Human nature is not fixed. Our nature is driven by will. Everyone has the ability to drive nature, but their results depend on the direction of their will. A realist portrait painter, for example, often works off the current form of the world. They draw what they see, what is. They aren't necessarily independent value creators. But artists do have the potential to create so much new value if they choose. They have massive amounts of power to escape from life's

mundane and allow for human will to create purpose for life. I believe that is the core concept of
value.

I wonder, why has atheism become so widespread
today while the wilderness maintains a strong spiritual presence in many people's lives? Perhaps God
is not capable of clear communication. Perhaps
modern science has influenced modern scholars in
a way that makes religion unbelievable. But, without God, perhaps many people are still able to at-
tain a sense of purpose in life that is not provided
by religion. The power to create value provides an
exceptional source of purpose. Mountains can create an emotional draw for many people—the way
they tower over the earth, impervious to storms—
as symbols of strength. Where better to create value
than on a mountain?

In some religions, asceticism creates purpose
through a ticket to the afterlife. Self-discipline is
not seen as an end; it was always a means for creating purpose. Thus, climbing is not itself an end, but
rather a process.

People are often focused on what is common, and
that makes it hard to develop value. But what is
common is not necessarily intrinsic. The meaning
of something is what humanity gives it. By recog-
nizing that objective value does not exist in this
kind of world, one must either create their own val-

ue or fall into passive nihilism, which is when we do things without asking *why*.

When I climb mountains, I must carry burdens, equipment, weight—voluntary self-cruelty. I must reject the values that define comfort and stability. I must live close to the edge and create an inner drive to reach the summit. In a sense, climbing is my anti-religion. It does not prescribe moral rules. It is a form of my will. The end, the summit, the substance of life, is whatever I make of it.

I don't want to speak solely for myself, though. I made a post on an online climbing forum, hoping to hear from the community. I asked, "What makes climbing special? What kind of value can be created through climbing, and how is the danger justified?"

The responses overwhelmingly referred to the prospect of self-improvement. Many found value in the ability to endure, referencing moments of dehydration, fighting cold, forced to push through. The experience is humbling, which is important for some, but it also builds people up. There is no feeling like accomplishing a climb that has caused so much struggle. Even when we aren't successful on a climb, we must come to accept our failings—often a healthy perspective that we can carry into many aspects of life.

I can relate. Climbing did not come easy to me

when I was first introduced to the sport. First of all, I had a terrible fear of heights. It took a lot of exposure time to get comfortable. Moreover, I have an autoimmune disease called scleroderma, which affected growth in my left hand and arm when I was young. As a result, I have limited strength and range of motion in my left pointer finger and thumb. I struggle to move the joints on those fingers and can't use them for climbing. At first, I thought there was no way climbing could work for me. A number of people told me that I'd never be able to climb well. However, one of my climbing mentors flipped my perspective. He took one look at my left pointer finger, which is noticeably thinner than most fingers, and he said, "That's your crux finger!" He told me about a really thin finger crack that he struggled with because his fingers are big. The next day, I went to try the crack, and, sure enough, my finger did fit. I may not be able to grab much with that finger, but I can still jam it into cracks. This changed my outlook on my weakness. I realized it would be possible to adapt and overcome the difficulties that I faced.

It felt empowering to have eventually developed my own climbing style that only uses the three functional fingers on my left hand. Over the years, I adapted so well that I don't even think about how I'm going to grab left-handed holds anymore, because it became second nature. Funny enough, basic tasks like opening door knobs or holding utensils are still hard with my left hand. But I haven't been motivated to solve those boring problems; I just use my right hand.

On the online forum, one person reflected on the dangers of climbing in a particularly interesting way. They noted that the dangers have improved their calculated risk taking, which has increased their willingness to accept other appropriate risks in life. Overall, they were able to become a more confident person. On a similar note, an employee at a trauma hospital replied, "I've realized over a decade in this career that any person can have a life altering incident at any time." Every day risks— things like car crashes or strokes—can be managed, but not removed. The same goes for climbing. There are inherent risks, but risk shouldn't devalue the pursuit of joy.

Finally, the most touching response came from a friend of mine, Meredith, who was a counselor at a camp for kids battling cancer: "I've been working at a climbing wall specifically built for children with disabilities. I can't begin to tell you the change in self esteem for those kids after climbing just 40 feet. It has been incredible to foster their power through climbing. I was at the top of the wall a few weeks ago while a child was climbing up. He yelled to himself, 'I need to be brave!' I yelled back, 'You don't need to be brave, because you *are* brave.' He jumped straight into my arms when he reached the top. I said, 'Hey bud, guess what, you are brave!' The top of that tower is covered in sharpie from older campers, some still with us, some not, with messages about never giving into fear, never giving up—always jumping into the unknown. It's so powerful. I think things like that make climbing special. Once you conquer your greatest physical fear, everything gets easier. I think about how some of those kids go home and tell their nurses how fearless they were for climbing the wall. I hope they use that energy to fearlessly face the needles or the chemo. Climbing shows them the resilience they already had deep inside. Ableist people love telling disabled folks what they can and cannot do. But if someone ever tries to tell one of those kids that they can't do something, they can turn around and tell them to *F off*. If they can climb that wall, they can probably do whatever someone else says they can't."

Setback

After my fiasco with Liz, I took a couple weeks off from climbing to write and give Breezy some good attention. I knew I'd be going back to the Bugaboos soon, though. My longtime climbing partner, Luke, was coming up to British Columbia for his first Bugaboo trip, and we had a number of goals we wanted to tick.

Luke is one of the most sincere people I know. He never holds back his thoughts, whether agreeing or disagreeing. Most importantly, Luke always comes forward to talk through any sort of miscommunication. That's really important to me in a partner. Some people aren't candid about disagreements, but Luke genuinely wants to work things out when there is conflict. I'm the same way. Conflict between friends will always happen at some point. At those times, good communication is key. Especially in the mountains, it's essential you are on the same page as your partner, and Luke and I work well together in that way.

Luke is originally from Tennessee, but he went to university with me in Boston. Like me, after graduation, he went through a number of job changes, his ranging from firefighting in Washington to arborist work in Massachusetts, just trying to figure out what he wanted to pursue. After quitting his most recent job, Luke figured it would be a good time for a trip out west to clear his mind.

When I went to pick up Luke from the airport, I was feeling a little off. For some reason, my back and arms were aching, and I was having trouble with my temperature. At times, I was shivering in my puffy jacket, and then, randomly, I'd start sweating and need to turn up the A/C.

I was nervous about how I was feeling, but I downplayed it to Luke. I figured a good night's sleep would help, so we decided to take a day off before hiking into the Bugaboos.

After some rest, I began to feel well again, and I cruised up the approach trail to the Bugaboos with ease. Illness was no longer on my mind. Luke and I set up camp at Applebee, then planned our climb for the next day. We wanted to start off with a route close to camp so we wouldn't wipe ourselves out on the first day of climbing. We chose McTech Arete, a six pitch 5.10a on the nearby Crescent Spire.

The next morning, I woke up with a mild headache and sore throat. A few ibuprofen pills took the edge off, and I was good to go. Luke and I hiked across the Crescent Glacier for about 20 minutes, and we found ourselves at the bottom of a gorgeous crack system that continued up an exposed arete on the face of Crescent Spire.

Crescent Spire is far from the most inspiring mountain in the Bugaboos. It's really just a lump compared to its next door neighbor to the west, Bugaboo Spire. But what it lacks in prominence, Crescent Spire makes up for in route quality.

I led the first pitch, climbing up high-quality cracks to the top of a pillar. Then, Luke took the second pitch—the crux. He led up a thin, strenuous finger crack that split a steep face. I took the lead for the next two pitches, first clambering over some easy, blocky terrain, then up a stellar hand crack with two overhanging roofs to pull over.

As Luke led the fifth pitch, I started to feel some fatigue kicking in. Then, when I took the last pitch, I began feeling really sluggish. I knew it was odd for me to be so tired at that point, but I figured I just had a mild cold and it would all be fine if I got some good sleep that night and stuck it out for the rest of the trip. After topping out, then rappelling down to the base of the climb, I was smoked, but I tried my best to hide it from Luke.

Back at camp, I spent the rest of the afternoon laying on a rock, soaking in the high alpine sun, and I began to feel much better. Luke cracked open one of the beers he had packed and extended another out to me. I really wanted it, but reluctantly declined since I knew it wouldn't help my sickness. Luke and I talked about our options and decided to take the upcoming good weather window to attempt the Beckey-Chouinard route up South Howser Tower—a mega classic that we had been dreaming of climbing together for a while. The climb itself is a big undertaking at 5.10a with 15 pitches. Getting to the climb from Applebee is another big endeavor. We would have to hike across the Crescent Glacier, up a steep snow slope to the col between Bugaboo and Snowpatch Spires, then across the Vowell Glacier, drop down a steep slope behind Pigeon Spire, then across another glacier to the East Creek Basin, where the Beckey-Chouinard route begins.

We woke up at 1 am, opting to hike the approach in the dark so we could climb with daylight. The sun was up by the time we got to the East Creek Basin, and it became evident that our weather window might have been a little too optimistic. Clouds were forming overhead, and it was hard to tell what was going to come of them. Instead of committing to the route, we decided to hang out at the base of the climb to see what the clouds were going to do.

Things didn't change much after a couple of hours, so we decided to go for it. We started climbing, but the clouds didn't clear up. After my experience several weeks prior, I was more reluctant than usual, as we really did not want to end up in a storm up there. At the top of pitch three, Luke and I stopped to weigh our options. After a minute of staring at the next pitch ahead of us, Luke turned to me and said, "I'm not really feeling this right now."

Without hesitation, I replied, "Okay then, no worries. Let's bail."

It can be tough to turn around after such a long approach, but that's part of the reality of climbing in the alpine. Success is only special because failure is likely. These climbs are hard, there's a lot of risk involved, and it's totally fair to call it when you're not feeling it. One of the most important parts of climbing safely is being in the right headspace. If things don't feel right, turn around.

Just as we set up to rappel back down, we felt the first pellets of hail hitting our helmets. The weather had decided to come through after all, and we got the hell off that mountain with no reservations.

We took the next day off to rest, which I was grateful for because my sore throat was beginning to worsen. Despite the throat, however, I was feeling pretty well overall. I actually felt like I was in the best climbing shape I had ever been in. I was moving efficiently. I felt strong, well-balanced, and confident climbing in the mountains.

We had time for one more climb the next day before Luke had to head home. I really wanted to climb Snowpatch Spire, and our route of choice up the mountain was Surfs Up, 5.9.

Snowpatch Spire is a sight to behold. It's steep and tall from every aspect. The crack systems draw marvelous stripes up the granite walls. It's truly a rock climber's dream mountain.

Surfs Up is nothing to write home about for the first four easy and chossy pitches. But the final three pitches up incredible, long granite cracks to the summit make the route well worth it. I felt great all the way up to the top. Climbing the route felt like a cake walk, and I was all smiles until we rappelled back down. Back at the bottom, I crashed. I don't know what happened, but all my energy suddenly left me. Every step was wrenching, and my head was throbbing. I had to get back to camp to lay down.

I started rushing back toward Applebee while Luke

lagged behind. He yelled out to me, "Hey! Ari! Wait up!"

I stopped and realized how irresponsible it was to go off like that. My mind was no longer thinking logically. I was shivering. My body was shutting down. I was way too sick to be up there.

I eventually got back to camp, feeling totally wasted, but, by morning, I was feeling well enough to hike out. By the time we picked up Breezy from her doggie sleepaway camp in the nearby town of Invermere, I was feeling like I had a few days before—mild sore throat, but fine overall. Breezy jumped into my arms when she first saw me again, and I couldn't believe how long our five days apart had felt. She then dropped to the floor and opened up her arms, begging for belly rubs. I was happy to deliver.

The next stop was Calgary to drop off Luke at the airport. We congratulated each other on a great trip and said our goodbyes, then Luke headed back to his family's home in Tennessee. From there, I was planning to drive about 10 hours to Squamish to meet up with Kelsey, who I hadn't seen since The Swell.

About two hours into the drive, I noticed that my sore throat was getting worse, and I was having trouble swallowing. The aches and pains I had felt the previous week were back, and I was feeling especially fatigued. Still convinced I had a cold and had just overdone it in the Bugaboos, I kept driving until I reached the town of Golden. At that point, my throat was so swollen that I was drooling, and breathing was becoming uncomfortable. Worried about an airway emergency, I detoured to the hospital in Golden.

I walked into the hospital and could hardly speak to the nurse who came to assist me. Every word that came out was painful. Eventually, they gave me some steroids, which helped clear my airway, and some other medications to manage the pain. Unfortunately, a blood test revealed that I was positive for mononucleosis, which was surely going to throw a wrench in my plans for Squamish. But what I didn't realize was just how large of a toll the illness would take.

What I hadn't known was that my liver and spleen were quite swollen. Had I taken a fall in the Bugaboos, I could've risked rupturing either of the organs, which would have been life-threatening in such a remote location. The doctor was insistent that I refrain from any physical activity until my labs indicated my liver function was back to normal. She estimated about six weeks. At that point, I couldn't imagine going six weeks without climbing, but, the next morning I could hardly imagine doing anything.

I left the hospital feeling well-medicated and disappointed. I called up my parents to let them know that I was sick, and my dad convinced me to book a flight east so I could rest up at their house in Vermont. By the time I was on the plane the next morning, I was in severe pain. My muscles ached so much that I was hardly able to carry Breezy in her little pet carrier through the airport. I felt miserably sick through the whole flight.

My dad picked me up from the airport in Hartford, Connecticut at 2 in the morning, and he could tell I wasn't alright. I couldn't get any food down my throat, and I had to lean forward in order to open my airway enough to breath. After a three-hour drive, we got back to my parents' house in Vermont, where I was able to sleep for an hour before I woke up dry-heaving. I left Breezy behind with my mom, and my dad drove me to the emergency room.

I spent the next three days in the hospital in complete misery. The swelling in my liver and spleen had gotten worse, and laying down was uncomfortable—though that was all I could really do. Sleep didn't happen much. Even at night, when I tried my best to sleep, I was woken every few hours for my next dose of steroids and pain meds.

Of course, I wondered how I got the virus that caused my illness. Honestly, I don't know. My friends didn't hesitate to pick on me because mono is well-known as the kissing disease (the virus that commonly causes it is often spread through saliva). But, truth be told, you don't get a lot of action when your bedroom is in the back of a pickup truck.

After a few days, I was released from the hospital, and I was greeted by an ever excited Breezy at the front door of my parents' place. I was still so fatigued that I had to rely on my parents to walk her for the next week, but I was tremendously happy to have her by my side while I rested at home.

The reality hit hard. A week before, I had been climbing at my best, then, suddenly, I couldn't even walk up a flight of stairs. All I could do was lay in bed and wait. It was a wild crash down from peak physical fitness to pathetic couch potato.

After a week, I was able to walk Breezy again for about ten minutes at a time. After a few weeks, I was comfortable doing most things around the house, but my endurance was still pitiful, and my liver and spleen were still at risk of rupturing so I couldn't do any physical activity. At that point, I was at least well enough to fly back to Alberta to drive my truck back to my parents' place in Vermont for the rest of my down time.

Finally, after six weeks, I was climbing easy boulder problems in the gym again. I could tell it was going to take a bit to rebuild my strength and balance. Then, after nearly two months, in mid-October, I was so restless that I needed to hit the road again. My fitness was still not fully restored, but I was mentally more than ready to get back after it, and I had a big goal in mind to earn my fitness back.

The Shadow

I was in high school when I first saw an Ansel Adams photo of Half Dome, *Monolith*. I was captivated by the image, absolutely blown away by the massive vertical wall. Black granite streaks stretch along the height of its face, and its elevated position looming above Yosemite Valley, nearly 9,000 feet high at the summit and 4,000 feet above the valley floor, just adds to the impressive scale of Half Dome.

I had never been to Yosemite, but I immediately decided that I needed to go there after seeing that photo. I knew I'd need to stand on top of Half Dome someday. At the time, I wasn't a climber, so I had no clue it was possible to climb up the sheer Northwest Face. I didn't know anyone could even climb walls of comparable height. I figured I would hike up the back side—like a *normal* person.

If you haven't seen Half Dome, it looks just as the name implies—a vault cut down the middle with a missing half. One side is a convex slope of smooth granite, the other a 2,000 foot vertical wall. Most people who make it to the top hike about eight miles from the valley floor to the summit, topping out on the upper slopes of Half Dome with cables installed into the slab for hikers to hold onto for safety. However, I lost interest in the idea of hiking up Half Dome once I learned how to climb.

The hiking route is often crowded, and I'm not particularly inspired by the industrial cable installation. The cables are a good thing for most people, since the end of the trail is particularly steep up slick rock. I imagine there would be a lot more accidents without them. But, in my mind, the most interesting way to get up Half Dome would be climbing the Northwest Face.

The Northwest Face of Half Dome was first climbed in 1957 by Royal Robbins, Mike Sherrick, and Jerry Gallwas—an historic achievement in climbing. At the time, it was the longest rock climbing route of its kind to be ascended in the United States. Due to its significance, the route was included in the *50 Classics*. It is a classic, indeed, and one of the most beautiful routes I have ever seen.

Yosemite Valley is pretty much the epicenter of *big wall* climbing in North America. A climbing route is typically classified as a big wall if it takes most climbers more than one day to complete it. Climbers will usually sleep on ledges along the way. If there are no ledges big enough to accomodate a night's sleep, climbers need to use a hanging platform called a portaledge. However, advancements in skill and equipment have allowed climbers to really up the ante. Now, the best of the best can climb big walls in a matter of hours. But, for most, two days is standard for climbing Half Dome.

Since there are no resupply stops along the way, big wall climbers need to carry all of their food, water, and waste up the wall with them. With big, heavy loads, we ditch the backpacks and instead trail a rope behind us to haul our gear using a pulley after climbing each pitch. It's exhausting work.

After a long drive to California, I was so eager to get up on the walls that I almost forgot I'd hardly been climbing in months. I dropped Breezy off with a few friends in San Francisco, where she was immediately spoiled with new toys, treats, and attention from her sitters. I gave the little punk a big hug, then drove the four hours east to Yosemite Valley.

I pulled into the parking lot of Half Dome Village, a little collection of shops and campgrounds, where

I had plans to pick up my climbing partner, Marc. The last text message I'd gotten from him said he would be in Half Dome Village sneaking into the campground showers for a rinse. Knowing Marc, it was much appreciated, because I'm sure he desperately needed a shower. Marc truly fits the description of the hippie dirtbags of Yosemite lore.

Yosemite has a strong history of dirtbaggery. Back in the days of Royal Robbins, when Yosemite big wall climbing was starting to boom, Camp 4 (the main walk-in campground) was filled with nonconformists who gave up standard luxuries to live in Yosemite Valley and climb full-time. Many were dedicated to the craft of first ascents and ultimately became the icons of dirtbaggery. Over the years, the glorification of these dirtbag climbers morphed that otherwise unflattering dirtbag designation into a badge of honor.

There he is. There was no mistaking Marc. I saw him walking toward my truck barefoot. His long, wet hair hung down his back. Who knows when he last had a haircut? He wore a t-shirt that was two sizes too large. I am sure he got it for free somewhere, and it was probably the only shirt he had with him in the Valley.

Marc hopped up into my truck and was quick to share in utter excitement, "Dude, I scored so much free food in Camp 4 last night from a group that

was on their way out. We'll be set all week!" Later
that night, Marc could be found walking around
Camp 4 with his newly acquired tote of food, offer-
ing up free snacks in exchange for a place to sleep
in other campers' sites so he wouldn't have to pay
for his own campsite. Marc is the kind of guy who
is willing to do almost anything to keep the dirtbag
dream alive, and I really look up to him for that
passionate dedication to his adventurous lifestyle.

The first time Marc and I went on a trip together,
we thru-hiked the Long Trail from Massachusetts
to Canada. Since then, we'd developed a history of
taking on long challenges together. The last time
we had climbed together was a little over a year
before this Yosemite trip. We climbed all day at
Smith Rock in Oregon, then we drove straight to
Mount Hood, where we climbed the Cooper Spur,
a very steep snow climb on the north side of Hood,
starting at 11 pm that night. Between Smith Rock
and Hood, we climbed for 30 hours without sleep,
only taking a short break on the drive between the
two. I can always count on adventure when Marc
is around, and he was the perfect partner for the
Northwest Face of Half Dome.

The next morning, we had our bags packed: two
ropes, two sets of cams and nuts, harnesses, climbing shoes, helmets, nearly enough carabiners to
hold the keys for every apartment in San Francisco,
various slings, pulleys and other technical equip-

ment for big wall climbing, plastic bags with kitty litter for poop (obviously shitting off a cliff onto climbers below is hygienically unacceptable), a durable bag to carry our waste in, toilet paper, sleeping bags, a few jackets, ample granola bars for two days, and three gallons of water.

The approach to Half Dome with heavy bags is a challenge on its own. I found it more terrifying than the actual climb. There are two ways to get to the bottom of the route: you can go the safer but agonizingly long way by hiking on a trail around the entire backside of Half Dome, or you can take the direct, much more dangerous approach up the *Death Slabs*—steep rock slopes beneath the face of Half Dome. Marc and I chose the Death Slabs approach because it is roughly six miles shorter than the other trail. Hiking even a short distance with our heavy gear and water loads was already agonizing enough.

The two biggest hazards on the Death Slabs are the fixed lines and the position under a rockfall zone. Since the slabs are so steep, there are often fixed ropes tied to trees above the steepest and blankest sections. Climbers can clip ascending devices to the ropes to climb up them. These ropes are only maintained by the stewardship of other climbers, and they aren't recognized by the National Park Service. Thus, a meddling rodent could possibly chew through one of the anchors, or a falling rock could

slice a rope, but the damage might not be notice-
able from below. People have died on these fixed
lines when unseen damage caused a rope to break
while a climber was ascending it. To reduce the
risk, Marc and I made things a little more difficult
for ourselves. We free climbed up the slabs with our
ascenders on the fixed lines next to us as backups,
delicately smearing on slippery granite with heavy
bags on our backs. If we slipped while climbing the
slabs, our ascenders, which were attached to our
harnesses with a sling, would catch on the fixed
ropes and stop our fall (so long as the ropes held).
We felt a lot better by not putting any direct weight
on the ropes, and, luckily, neither of us needed to
test them as our backup protection. Fortunately for
any climbers coming up after us, the lines appeared
to be in good shape when we got to the top of them.

The other hazard was one we could not mitigate:
rockfall. Given the funnel shape of the slabs, it
was possible for any falling rock to crush us. There
wasn't much of an escape path, so, if a big chunk of
Half Dome decided to break off, which had actually happened a few years before, we undoubtedly
would have been killed. To make things even more
unsettling, we heard reports of a thousand-pound
death block that was teetering back and forth on a
route that went up the center of the face above us.
Looking up, I could see the block, a huge, triangu-
lar boulder, the size of a small house, that looked
like it was about to shear off the side of the wall.

The spookiest part about the triangle was that there was absolutely nothing holding it up from below. The bottom edge of the triangle was a roof created by a section of rock that had fallen out from below it. The other two sides of the triangle were visible fractures in the rock, and it looked like it was being held up by its acute little point at the top. Apparently, the crack at the bottom of the triangle used to be the width of a knifeblade, but, over time, had widened to a couple inches. I imagined what it would sound like if that thing came down. Every step I took was followed by a glance up to make sure the block was still in its place, levitating above us. Finally, when we got to the bottom of the wall, we were able to move out from underneath that death triangle to the base of our route, which was far off to the left, comfortably out of the way of that frightening block.

I was wiped by the time Marc and I finished the approach. I could definitely feel the toll of the months I had spent healing. My legs were certainly weaker than they had been earlier that summer, and my general fitness had fallen well behind. I was frustrated by my exhaustion, but hopeful that I could build my strength back quickly by pushing through this climb.

We spent the night sleeping at the base of the wall, alarms set for a 5 am start. I figured I was pretty good at sleeping anywhere, so I'd left my sleeping pad behind to save space in my bag. I struggled to get comfortable on my gravel bed, and I'm sure my restlessness was magnified by my excitement as I laid on my back looking up at the vast granite wall towering overhead. It stretched into the starry sky above, illuminated by a faint glow from the little remaining twilight. It was hard to imagine questing up that wall. Nevertheless, our quest began first thing in the morning.

Waking up at 5 am at the base of a climb never feels like waking up at 5 am when I'm at home. I almost find it impossible to drag myself out of a warm, cozy bed first thing in the morning, but I'm jazzed when my alarm goes off right before I'm about to go up a climb. There was very little to do to get ready. All of our gear was already sorted at the base of the route, and I had slept in the clothes that I would climb in. I ate a protein bar and energy gel for breakfast, and I was all set to go.

Marc and I moved quickly up the first few pitches up Half Dome. We were feeling confident, but we still had a long way to go. In total, the route usually takes about 23 pitches, and the hardest climbing was still well above us.

At around pitch six, I noticed my footing felt particularly off. A combination of under-exercised legs and under-utilized balance from my recovery had an apparent effect on my stability. Every move I made felt insecure, which is not what you want on Yosemite granite, which I found to be slicker than the other granite climbing areas I was used to.

I stepped onto a small sloping bump, then reached up as high as I could to get my hand onto another sloping ledge. I could feel myself struggling, and I noticed that my left knee didn't feel stable with my foot on that sloping bump. Suddenly, I fell. The route had gone around a corner, so Marc and I were out of sight from one another. Marc had to belay, paying out slack in the rope by feel, which is a skill I'm glad Marc had mastered. Out of nowhere, he heard me yell, "Falling!" I felt my right foot impact on a ledge below me, right before the rope came tight and I came to a stop, dangling from a small nut I had wedged into an awkwardly shaped crack. It wasn't a great placement, but it was the best I could do to protect that move. I was relieved and a little surprised it held. I hung there for a moment and felt a quick surge of pain in my ankle. It wasn't anything serious—probably a minor sprain from the impact of my fall.

Marc called up to me. "Are you alright?"

"Yeah, I banged my ankle a little, but I think it's okay. Just give me a minute." I was startled from the fall. I really shouldn't have fallen there. The move wasn't any harder than 5.9. I began to doubt whether I could pull off this route. Maybe I was far too eager to climb something big without easing back into climbing. Perhaps I didn't respect the limits of my body after coming back from illness. I wondered if I was asking for trouble.

"Do you want to come down?"

For some reason, I felt a surge of motivation. After all, I knew I could climb that pitch. Even given my poor conditioning, it was still a freak fall. I got back on the wall and kept going. The discomfort in my ankle amplified the uneasiness in my balance, but I really didn't want to fall again. I pressed my hands into the rock like they were covered in glue and slowly moved my way upward. The rock began to look featureless as I climbed higher above the nut I had fallen on. I wouldn't be able to get another piece of protection in until the top of the pitch. I *really* didn't want to fall again. I took a deep breath, put trust in my wobbling legs, and made it to the top of the pitch without falling again.

Despite that moment of doubt, the climbing ahead went smoothly. Our goal was to make it to Big Sandy Ledge to bivy that night. Big Sandy, at the top of pitch 17, is the only flat ledge on the route that's big enough for a couple of people to sleep on. But our momentum started to slow as we hit the double-digit pitches, and it became apparent that we wouldn't make it before nightfall. We pulled out our headlamps, ready to continue in darkness.

Due to the northwest aspect, we spent the whole day climbing in the shadow of Half Dome. It was terribly cold. I found myself shivering at every belay, even while wearing a long sleeve base layer, a fleece, and two puffy jackets. But, one hour before sunset, the sun finally crept around the corner of the wall and provided a brilliant ray of warmth. It was short-lived, as the sun continued beneath the horizon and the frigid darkness took over.

The cold kept us moving, though, and I found the delayed evening sunshine to be rather metaphoric. You have to keep climbing, moving to stay warm, in order to make it. It's like any kind of pursuit— whether searching for happiness, love, or truth—in that you can't just sit there and wait for it to come to you. You have to get out and seek it. Of course, that sun will come around eventually anyway, but do you really want to sit around in the cold just waiting for that single hour of light?

A thought came to me as the sun came around the corner. For the first time all day, I saw my shadow. That meant I had been facing the sun all day, even though the wall provided shelter from the sun's rays. The sun, in philosophy, has often been a symbol for truth. It may be more comfortable to stand with your back to the sun, but then your path onward is cast in shadow. When you walk facing the sun, your silhouette is traced behind as you continue forward. Despite the cold, I was grateful the shadow of the wall relieved the stress of facing the sun all day. But I also recognized that this wall was one more obstacle that needed to be overcome in order to really face the sun again.

Our pace came to a sudden halt on pitch 12. This pitch passes a big section of the route that had been lost in a rockfall a few years before. What used to be a pitch of 5.9 was now a blank face, which could only be navigated with an awkward knot toss technique.

Marc and I had read a little about the knot toss on a climbing forum, but there wasn't a whole lot of information about it since the obstacle was fairly new to the route. Some comments described it as *amusing*, others said it was *straightforward*. I was hardly convinced this mid-route engineering would be straightforward, but we'd figured we would wing it when we got there.

It was twilight. I led up to a fixed bolt that I was able to clip into for support. I leaned back in my harness and peered around a corner, shining my headlamp across a blank face, and saw a big crack that led into a wide chimney for the next two pitches. I just needed to figure out how to get over there.

I pulled up a section of the haul rope, which was trailing behind me from the back of my harness, and tied a big overhand knot. The haul rope is used at the end of every pitch so the leader can haul up the bags while the follower climbs. But, for the time being, the haul line would stand in as an improvised grapnel. I gave the knot a good toss, hoping to get it caught in the crack, but I didn't even come close. I realized this was going to be much harder than I had hoped. I tossed the knot a dozen times. I swung back and forth to try getting closer. I even tried to pendulum all the way over to the crack. I had no luck. Soon my tosses became reckless, as I desperately fired the knot at the crack in frustration. Finally, the knot sunk into the crack, but, just as I pulled on the rope, it slipped right out. The sky was now completely dark, and I hung in my harness with my head down. I was breathing heavily, exhausted. I felt lost, dangling in space, only able to see what was within the beam of my headlamp. I gave the knot toss a few more tries, but realized I was too tired to throw the knot deliberately, so I had Marc lower me back down to the belay for a rest.

Marc offered to go up, and I was hopeful he would have better luck. Where I left off, Marc started swinging around, tossing the rope across the wall and into darkness. He took a break after a number of fruitless attempts, and I could tell he was pretty tired too. This roadblock was severely bringing down our motivation. Marc brought up bailing as an option, but we realized that it would be too risky to rappel in the dark, since we did not know if we'd find any fixed anchors right below us. We would have likely needed to leave a lot of our gear behind.

At this point, we both wanted to sleep, and we were a bit resentful that our belay was on such a small ledge, barely big enough for one person to stand. Marc said half jokingly, "Okay, let's just wait out the night and we'll bail in the morning. We can pass the time by trying to land this knot toss, but, if we don't get it by sunrise, then I'm going down!" Then, as if some otherworldly force heard Marc's cry, he managed to nail the knot toss on his next try. With the knot firmly stuck in the crack, Marc was able to pull himself over to the start of the next pitch and we were ready to blast off again.

At 2 am, after 21 hours of climbing, we made it to Big Sandy Ledge. Let me tell you, I was well past grumpy. I think Marc said something to me when we got there, but I ignored him completely in my drowsy state. Upon crawling onto Big Sandy, I pulled out my sleeping bag, tied myself to an anchor, and immediately passed out, laying just inches from the edge of the cliff. Five hours later, I woke up to the sound of people talking above me. I rubbed my puffy eyes and looked up to find a pair of legs hanging over the edge of the cliff. I couldn't believe how far we had come. The top of Half Dome was right there, just six pitches away. I stretched out, relieving the aches throughout my body. This was going to be a long six pitches.

Marc and I continued upward, but our speed was quickly slowed by the increasingly strenuous climbing. We certainly weren't making record time on the route, but we kept a respectable pace. As we approached pitch 21, I could feel butterflies in my stomach. Pitch 21 is the notorious Thank God Ledge. A photo of this ledge was seen by the world on the cover of *National Geographic* when Alex Honnold famously free soloed the route. I still remembered when that issue of *National Geographic* arrived at my parents' house when I was in high school. The photo showed Honnold standing on the narrow Thank God Ledge with his back pressed against the slightly overhanging wall, no ropes or harness to be seen. At the time, I wasn't much of a climber and had never heard of Alex Honnold. I'd held the magazine cover up to my mom and asked, "Why the hell would anyone walk out onto that ledge without a safety net below them?" I never read the article, so little did I know that he'd actually climbed a route up the whole face that I would attempt one day.

Thank God Ledge is about 35 feet long and two feet wide when you first get on it, but it narrows to less than a foot wide in the middle of the traverse. Climbing across it isn't actually difficult. After all, it's just a ledge. But it's one *scary* ledge. The exposure in that particular spot can be pretty overwhelming, and the wall behind the ledge overhangs in a way that makes you feel like it's pushing you off. Some people choose to do a sideways shuffle walk across the ledge, but I had so much gear clipped to the back of my harness that I was worried I wouldn't be able to get my back pressed up against the wall enough to feel secure. Furthermore, I was still feeling off balance in my current condition. I opted, instead, to do a rather pathetic, slow crawl across the ledge. There were two problems with this decision. First, my face was pointed downward the whole time, so the vertical drop below looked even more dramatic. The phrase *don't look down* did not work in that stance. Secondly, I would eventually have to stand up again at the end of the ledge to get into the next section of vertical climbing. Crawling across the ledge was terrifying enough. I was nearly in tears as the weight of my cams felt like they were pulling me off into the abyss below. Standing up again on tired legs with about a foot of ledge to balance on was certainly the scariest part of the climb. I felt like I was cemented down on my hands and knees. Every time I started to stand up, I would quickly give up and plant myself back down on the ledge.

Marc called over to me, "You've got this!"

"I'm losing my mind a little." I was being completely overdramatic. I just had to stand up. I am no stranger to exposure, but my poor balance at the time was really limiting my feeling of security. I closed my eyes, took a deep breath, and reminded myself to find my zone. It is wild what a simple breath can do. One thing I've always been good at is pushing through uncomfortable moments and finding focus whenever climbing feels scary. Intentional breathing has always helped me do this.

I stood up slowly, made the next move, and anchored myself in comfortably so I could haul the bags and Marc could follow. I was impressed to see Marc effortlessly shuffle across the ledge like a circus performer on a tightrope. In hindsight, I really shouldn't have hesitated as much as I had. Marc made it look as easy as it should've been. At least those moments of overcoming fear, even if the fear is unnecessarily exaggerated, are healthy practice.

Just a few more pitches and we would be done. Marc took the lead for the remaining bit, hoping to take us to the top before sunset. He was a little faster than me at leading, and I was a little bit faster at following traversing terrain, which requires some tricky techniques while self-belaying. Since Marc would be hauling the bags while I followed, it was much more efficient for me to belay myself along the rope while I climbed instead of waiting for him to belay me from above. This style isn't the most graceful, but it is a huge time saver on big walls when hauling is involved.

I felt a huge wave of relief as I saw Marc disappear

out of sight over the edge and onto the top of Half Dome. We were so exhausted, but, finally, our adventure was complete—sort of. We still needed to get down. Nevertheless, Half Dome was in the bag. I followed the pitch just as the sun was setting. The Valley was cast in a gorgeous golden glow, and I no longer felt the cold shadow of the Northwest Face dominating me. We looked out at the fading alpenglow and paused for a moment of congratulations.

Unfortunately, we were not able to savor the moment for too long. We were quick to get our gear packed up right before the sky turned black, then we began the slow nine-mile hike off the backside of Half Dome down to the Valley below. Every mile or so, I had to stop to sit down and take the weight off my legs. At one point, I was ready to quit, crawl into the woods, and call it a night. But my saving grace was a handful of chocolate-covered espresso beans that Marc offered me. I've always advocated carrying emergency chocolate. This time it really pulled through.

We finally got down to my truck around midnight, and I can't remember the last time I had been so grateful for sleep. The next morning, we washed up and stretched. We felt surprisingly good given how much we had just climbed. I was so happy that we'd made it up Half Dome, but I was admittedly a little disappointed in my overall performance on the route. I was not in the kind of shape I expected from myself. It's hard to accept when big goals need to go on the back burner in order to focus on improvement. That was a reality I had to accept at that point in time.

Dancing in the Desert

With the temperature forecasted to drop in Yosemite and my pup on my mind, I picked Breezy up from San Francisco and headed to the desert for the first time since June. This time we would head to Red Rock, Nevada—a world-class climbing destination right outside of Las Vegas.

I'd taken my second climbing trip ever to Red Rock, where I'd flailed my way up a few routes with little to no skill. I was excited to return as a much better climber, and I figured the relaxed nature of desert climbing would be ideal for focusing on building up my balance.

I met up with my friend Dan, who used to be Zephyr's housemate in Utah. He had recently quit his high-paying job as an aircraft engineer and was taking some time off to live in his truck and travel full-time. Dan had learned how to ice climb the previous winter, but he was just getting into rock climbing, so he was eager to follow me around, learn more about the gear, and get more comfortable on the rock. Fittingly, I took him up all of the routes I had attempted when I was a beginner at Red Rock. Not only were they good routes for Dan to cut his teeth on, but I was also curious to see how different they would feel climbing them again a number of years later with a lot more mileage under my belt. Specifically, there were two climbs that I couldn't wait to repeat: Straight Shooter, 5.10a and Olive Oil, 5.7 R.

Straight Shooter is a beautiful, dead-straight finger crack that runs up a steep sandstone slab covered in a gorgeous, smoky black varnish. It's a short route, but the fingers are tight and the feet are difficult for short people like me (I'm just under 5'7"). The crux is the thinnest part of the crack, about halfway up, where the foot placements are little chips in the stone far out on the face to either side of the crack. I once saw a six-foot-tall woman climb through the crux in one move, quickly reaching the secure hand holds that allow for a great rest after the crux. But the crux took me a few moves, and it required me to spread my legs far to either side for secure footing. It was a great route for me to build confidence in my balance again.

I thought back to the first time I had tried that route. At the time, it was way out of my league, so I took a number of falls and had to pull on cams to get past the crux. But, this time, I flew up the route with ease. It was a great confidence boost, which I needed since I'd taken that stupid fall on Half Dome.

Dan, on the other hand, didn't have so much luck with Straight Shooter. He was hardly able to do the first move and quickly wrote off climbing finger cracks. Fortunately, I knew he'd have a much better time on the next day's objective.

I was happy to have Breezy around again, so I wanted to bring her along on as many adventures as possible now that we were in a dog-friendly place. I knew that Olive Oil would be the ideal route to carry Breezy up and help Dan build his multi-pitch experience. Olive Oil is five pitches long. It's quite easy, but it does get runout in places. I've found easy runout climbing to be one of the best ways to feel bold again when confidence is otherwise low.

The first time I climbed Olive Oil was actually with Marc and our mutual friend, Jason. We took all day to navigate our way up its moderate five pitches. It was laughable how long it took us to do that climb. This time around, it would be a lot more casual—so casual, in fact, that Breezy was coming along for the ride.

Of all the routes I've done over the years, Olive Oil has remained one of my favorites. It was exhilarating to blast up that thing with Breezy in my backpack. Her head rested on my shoulder most of the way, and she never even flinched when she looked down at the ground hundreds of feet below. The route follows a wall of numerous incut jugs. Imagine grabbing the rims of big bowls the entire way up. It felt incredibly secure, but there weren't many places to put protection. I blasted up each pitch, and Dan followed eagerly. The day before, Dan had mentioned that he was uncomfortable with the idea of hanging from an anchor without a ledge to stand on. Olive Oil has one hanging belay on it, and Dan was thrilled to hang off it and feel safe—huge progress for him. I was just happy to have led up that thing so easily. Obviously, I knew I had improved, but it was meaningful to actually experience my vast improvement by reflecting on the last time I had climbed that route. Markers of improvement like that are meaningful in many aspects of life, especially in a craft I've been so immensely passionate about for years. I think it goes without saying that, with passion and drive, comes growth and self-improvement.

That night Dan and I found ourselves listening to music and cooking dinner in our campsite, which was off the beaten path on public land. We were never ones to pay for campgrounds like the popular site right across from Red Rock. There is so much amazing public land that's free and open for camping if you're willing to explore a little. Our spot was tucked away, surrounded by Joshua trees. There was nobody in sight, and the classic desert sky was speckled with incredible stars.

Breezy would do this weird thing at night in the desert where she would stay in one spot, pick a direction, and would just stare off into the darkness. Dan and I couldn't break her focus, so I picked her up and carried her over to join the little party that we were throwing.

Dan gave me a mischievous look as he changed the song playing out of his portable speakers. Suddenly, the Hora was blasting at full volume. Dan pointed to his camp chair, and I immediately broke out laughing. I dropped Breezy into the camp chair and bent down to grab a chair leg. Up she went as Dan and I danced and bobbed Breezy up and down. It was clear that the night had unexpectedly turned into a celebration of good times, good health, and the amazing desert wilderness we were so lucky to be living in that night.

When the song ended, we let Breezy down, and she quickly ran back to her spot to continue staring off in her direction of choice. I declared the occasion Breezy's Bat Mitzvah. "She's a woman! Oh how they grow up so fast!" I joked. Breezy wasn't so into the fun, but Dan and I kept the tunes coming, and soon our dancing escalated into floundering freestyle moves.

After dancing myself out, I took a break to sit on my tailgate. It occured to me that I didn't remember ever having that much fun dancing without alcohol involved. On one hand, it was a little sad to be one of two sober guys dancing like idiots in the middle of the desert. But, thinking back to my nights in Boston nursing bottles of whiskey, I was proud of myself for finding that kind of joy while partying without alcohol.

I'd stopped drinking when I was sick because my liver was in no condition to handle alcohol, even long after my major symptoms faded. But, a couple months later, despite my liver function returning to normal, I didn't feel compelled at all to buy myself any booze. If there was anything positive I could take away from my illness, it was that it got me through the process of quitting alcohol, which I had not been able to handle on my own before. In that moment, thinking back to how much it affected my health, I felt rather repulsed by the idea of drinking.

That night, with the coinciding realization about my subsided relationship with alcohol, was one of the most significant nights in my life. I've doubted my path so many times. It's easy to doubt your course of life when you think like me—never satisfied with norms, always seeking extremes far outside of societal expectations. These feelings are not a choice; they are driven by the core of my emotions. If I had a say in the matter, I would've just kept things simple. I wouldn't have needed to doubt whether I was doing the right thing by risking my life in the mountains.

There, in the desert, I came to terms with the answer to the question that had been looming over me all summer: *Was I wasting my time by living on the road and spending all of my time climbing?* No. I knew that, if I could feel that free from my demons, I was, without a doubt, doing the right thing for myself. I've lived in Vermont, Boston, California, and many places in between, but I had never been so content living anywhere other than in my truck in that spot in the desert that night.

Alone

Things started to slow down a bit as autumn progressed. I made my way up to Moab, Utah to make the most of cooler climbing weather in the desert. In the fall, Moab becomes a base camp for climbers from all over the world. The desert nights often drop below freezing, the general tourist population decreases, and the town quiets down a bit. But the daytime temperatures are usually great for climbing—sunny and comfortable, but cool enough for good grip on the rock.

Moab, the central hub of *Canyon Country*, is surrounded by vast public lands where nomads can set up camp for free. There is a seemingly endless amount of sandstone walls to climb near town, but the real crown jewel is an hour's drive southwest in the northern part of Bears Ears National Monument known as Indian Creek.

The Creek, as it's called, is world-renowned for its crack climbs. The routes follow distinct cracks that split blank walls. The technique requires jamming and twisting hands, arms, feet, legs, or whatever body parts will fit into the cracks. There aren't many holds outside of the cracks in the Creek, so it's a good place to test proper crack climbing techniques.

I spent a few days climbing in the Creek, often linking up with friends I had met in passing on my travels. A nice thing about Indian Creek in the fall is that it draws climbers from all over, so it was pretty easy to run into people I knew. But the caveat is that the Creek gets crowded, especially on weekends, so it's not an ideal place to get some alone time.

I'm good at acting gregarious, but, deep down, I'm an introvert. Crowds get overwhelming fast, and too much socializing can be exhausting. After a long summer of rock climbing, I needed a little bit of alone time.

Climbing alone can be pretty limiting. I do enjoy free soloing, climbing without a belay, but I only free solo well below my limit. At a maximum, I'll free solo 5.8. However, there is another way to climb alone—rope solo climbing, a dark art that requires some obscure techniques. Very few climbers really know how rope soloing works, and even fewer ever try it.

Rope soloing—giving oneself a belay—can often be a bit scarier than climbing with a normal partner belay. This is because your life is reliant on your own anchor-building craft and your own ropework without anyone else to check it for errors. Additionally, self-belaying is less precise, and a lot of slack can end up in the rope below, which can often lead to bigger falls. As if you already didn't want to fall enough, it's exaggerated by the fact that nobody else is around to rescue you. Even when I'm rope soloing, despite the increased risk management provided by the rope, I try really hard not to fall or make any mistakes.

I had been rope soloing for about a year at that point, and I had my techniques down pretty well. Nevertheless, it's a taxing system. First, I build an anchor at the bottom of the climb. If I'm lucky, there will be a big tree I can use. Otherwise, I have to use a bunch of cams and nuts. Since I won't be able to keep an eye on the gear, and since the belay will take the load of any falls, I often put four pieces in a rope solo anchor, where I might only put two or three in a normal climbing anchor. The other key is that all of the pieces need to be able to hold an upward pull since a rope solo anchor will be pulled upward if the leader falls. This is because a fall on a piece of protection above will cause a pulley effect, which turns the climber's fall down on one side of the rope into a pull upward on the other side. This is the same as when a belayer gets pulled up while catching a lead fall, except there's no belayer's body mass to assist with the catch.

Next, I clip one end of the rope to the anchor, then attach the rope to a self-belay device on my harness called the Silent Partner. The Silent Partner is no longer in production, because rope solo climbing is such a niche discipline that the manufacturer never sold enough to make it a viable product. I was lucky enough to get my hands on one before the used price of them skyrocketed. I paid retail price for it a few years back, but, since it's a one-of-a-kind product, used Silent Partners can now be found on eBay for seven times the original market price.

As I climb, rope feeds through the Silent Partner, and I can clip it to protection. Usually, it turns into a cluster of rope strands dangling below, because the rope comes up from the belay, back down through the Silent Partner, then back up to a backup knot clipped to my harness, then back down into a bag that the rope is organized into at the belay. Soloists have gotten into deep trouble after getting confused about which rope strand was attached to the anchor. In fact, people have climbed entire pitches while clipping the wrong strand, only to discover they were actually free soloing. Once I'm at the top of a pitch, I can build an anchor, then rappel down to clean my gear, then I need to climb the pitch again on top rope to start the next pitch. Essentially, rope soloing requires leading, rappelling, then following—all alone—just to climb one pitch. It's a great way to make things way harder than they need to be. But I'm always up for challenges, so I've found it appealing.

I had an interesting idea while looking for unclimbed routes on a remote cliff in Utah, a few hours from Moab, far from where climbers typically explore. I wanted to put up a first ascent alone from the ground up. It would be one thing to scope out a climb, find a way to hike to the top of the cliff, then rappel down and drill a bolted anchor on my own, but that's a pretty uninteresting way to develop routes. I was committed to the adventurous style of ground-up first ascents, and I wanted to see if I could do it on my own.

I was sworn to secrecy about the area I went to. I don't even know if it has a real name, but I started to call it the Dead Creek, since the approach path follows an unmistakable wash, a dry stream bed, which only flows with water on rare, extremely rainy days. The Dead Creek is the landmark I have to look for every time I drive into the spot. Otherwise, the climbing would be easy to miss since the wall is far enough off the road, surrounded by other cliffs, that it's not obvious which one is covered in freshly developed crack climbs. I've only heard of three other people developing routes on that wall—one is a close friend, and the other two are his friends.

I hiked up the Dead Creek carrying all the gear I would need to rope solo an unknown route and bolt an anchor. Normally the load would be split with a partner, but Breezy is not exactly the most helpful when it comes to carrying climbing gear. In my pack, I had a 70 meter rope, all of my cams (not knowing what sizes I would need for a route I hadn't picked out yet), my harness, climbing shoes, a helmet, specialty rope solo equipment, a drill, a couple expansion bolts, a hammer, and a wrench for bolt installation.

The hike in is spectacular. The Dead Creek passes piles of petrified wood—logs and fragments of dead trees that have turned to stone with time—a testament to the preserving powers of the desert.

The base of the wall begins at the top of a giant slope of rocky debris, which can be ascended by following a faint herd path that was eroded by the earliest first ascensionists at that cliff. Along the hike are miniature sandstone towers, naturally sculpted over time into narrow-bodied spires.

After reaching the wall, I began to look around. Cracks were endless, but many of them looked too

difficult for me to climb or already had anchors installed by the other developers. A few routes initial-
ly caught my eye, but I realized they wouldn't be safe
to rope solo because the rock quality at the base of
the cracks seemed exceptionally brittle, which was
not confidence-inducing for a solo anchor.

I wandered back and forth for about an hour, not
totally sure what I was looking for. But then I decided to go a little further around a corner I hadn't yet
explored past. There was no more beaten path in
the talus that the other developers had packed out.
The ground at the base of the cliff became insecure,
and I found myself nearly slipping down the long,
loose rubble slope—a sure disaster, as the scree
pile was nearly 500 feet long. Carefully, I made my
way around the corner and onto a flat spot, where
I threw my pack down to rest. I looked up and saw
a parallel-sided crack above me that looked like it
was about the width of my fist. It was on the inside
of a corner feature on the wall, and there was a perfect ledge, right at the end of the crack, so I could
easily stop to install a bolted anchor for retreat and
use by future climbers.

I was able to build a pretty solid ground anchor
for a rope solo. The rock quality was sturdy, but I
was only able to get small pieces into a thin crack.
Smaller cams and nuts are often more likely to
blow, since all the force makes contact with a very
small area of the rock. Right before starting up the

crack, I made a last-second decision to add a big cam to the anchor low in the same crack that I was going to climb. The downside to this decision is that I only had two other cams of that size. Since the crack was, for the most part, consistent in size, I was going to be limited in protection.

I climbed about half of the crack while bumping one cam above me the whole way. I found it to be fairly strenuous, because the crack was just barely wider than my fist. I was able to jam my fist in there loosely, but I had to keep it gripped tight, or else it would start to slip. The good news was that my feet fit in the crack perfectly, so at least they felt very secure.

About halfway up, I was able to take a nice rest in a pod that was big enough for me to jam my whole arm across it, pressing my hand into one side and my elbow into the other like a chicken wing. The pod took the next size cam, so for the first time on that route I was able to leave a second piece of protection behind. Moving higher, I was back down to the only two fist-sized cams. I left one a few moves above the pod, then continued to push the other up the crack with me as I climbed. I made a move, reached down and moved the cam higher, made another move, then repeated. The climbing got easier as I neared the top. The crack shrunk to the size of my hand, which was a much more comfortable fit. I was able to leave my last fist-sized cam behind and use a couple smaller cams to protect the finish. I pulled myself onto the ledge at the top of the route, unclipped the drill from my harness, and drilled two holes at eye level for a pair of bolts. As I drilled, the sandstone blew into my face, covering me in a reddish dust. It felt good to leave my mark up there, knowing I had accomplished my goal of establishing a ground-up solo first ascent.

This was far from one of my biggest achievements. It really wasn't too difficult. It was a short route and, in the grand scheme of things, it wasn't very impressive. After all, far bigger and bolder first ascents had been established solo by other climbers. Still, my new route was meaningful to me, and I didn't care what anyone else thought about it.

It was just me out there, climbing for myself, creating for myself without influence from anyone else. In the beginning, the whole reason I wanted to climb and write full-time was to escape the influence of society. Doing this route for myself, with nobody else watching, nobody making photos for me to share, reminded me why I became passionate about climbing in the first place. It was always about doing something that made me happy, even if I wasn't always able to articulate why that was. I may not have been happy at every moment along the way, but recurring moments of happiness have made climbing worth it.

I want to create things for other people, too. I don't want to live a selfish life. Facing dangerous mountains feels selfish enough. But it's not all about my personal gains. I've learned that I can't have an earnest relationship with the other people in my life unless I am good to myself first. When I am intentional about the things I care about, then I can sincerely share my love with others. I think that is the core principle of value creation and self-fulfillment. It takes a lot of self-understanding to radiate one's own value. Without that personal depth, it's hard to differentiate honest personal value from the reflection of another person's value. When value shines from an intrapersonal sun, it can be a catalyst for passion, a prompt for motivation. This applies far beyond climbing. Without motivation, life seems stagnant.

The *dirt bag* lifestyle is popular in the climbing world. It's a symbol of freedom. Every year more people quit their jobs to live on the road and climb as much as possible. I've joked that homelessness is the new American dream. But even though I was sleeping in my truck and subsisting off potato chips, instant coffee and 50 cent ramen packs, I was homeless by choice. I am extremely privileged to have been able to make that choice.

In an ideal world, everyone, not just a privileged few, would be able to survive solely off of passion. I wish I could create that world. All I can really do is hope those with access to passion choose to emit it intentionally. This requires connecting with people from many different backgrounds and lending hands to those who struggle to incorporate the things that motivate them into their daily lives. If there is something I can do to make that possible for someone else, then I pledge to do all I can. The first step for people in my position is to listen.

For those looking to take a step in a new direction, to discover passion, start by asking, what is your *why*? Whether climbing, writing, creating, or working in any domain, an understanding of *why* you do something is a spark for motivation and success.

It is comforting to imagine there is something permanent about human beings, but humankind is always changing. This allows for self-fulfillment. It permits us to imagine meanings for life, whatever they are at each moment. Nevertheless, meaning is a simplification. Imposing our simplifications on others is what demonstrates human power. There is a danger to this power when it's used for oppression. But, at the same time, the imposition of simplifications allows knowledge and emotion to be spread healthily, so long as our simplifications are shared vigilantly. We can do more than just observe the beautiful scenery from high peaks; we can also create new routes, new goals.

Of course, climbing is not a catch-all answer to anything. I have certainly expressed that the climbing community is far from perfect. But I don't think you really love something without a willingness to be critical of it. Despite my range of criticisms and praises, for me, climbing has simply provided a healthy kind of emotion. It gives me a mode of creativity and expression. It is not about me being a great climber—I'm far from the greatest, after all—but it is about finding something that is deeply rooted inside me. It's about my passion for the sport. It's about a lifestyle that has played a major role in my existence. Most importantly, the path that climbing brought me down has taught me about transformation. Everyone is evolving every day, and we constantly have the potential to change with the right resources and drive.

On a mountain, you must climb quite a bit up and down to find your way. It's not supposed to be easy, and it is often scary. But this struggle provides an opportunity to be true to yourself. In the end, there is no single objective route up the mountain. There are winding trails, glaciers, and granite cracks that provide many different paths to the summit.

ACKNOWLEDGMENTS

First and foremost, thank you, Mom and Dad, for everything. Thanks to all the characters in this book and everyone else who joined me on these adventures. Thanks to the many friends that gave me couch and floor space to sleep on and storage space for my climbing gear for extended periods of time while I traveled the American west. Thanks to all the great dog sitters that took care of Breezy while I was in the mountains. Finally, thanks to everyone that I consulted for edits and feedback. This book would not have been the same without all of you.

Liz on Bugaboo Spire.

Luke in the Bugaboos.

Luke climbing on Snowpatch Spire.

Marc on the last pitch of Half Dome.

Marc leading on Half Dome.

Breezy enjoying the desert.

CPSIA information can be obtained
at www.ICGtesting.com
Printed in the USA
LVHW040120120319
610249LV00010B/28/P

9 781732 348233